The Swahili:
Idiom and Identity of an African People

The Swahili:
Idiom and Identity
of an African People

Alamin M. Mazrui
Ibrahim Noor Shariff

Africa World Press, Inc.
P.O. Box 1892
Trenton, New Jersey 08607

Africa World Press, Inc.
P.O. Box 1892
Trenton, NJ 08607

Cover and book design by Jonathan Gullery
This book is composed in Palatino

Library of Congress Cataloging-in-Publication Data

Mazrui, Alamin M.
        The Swahili : idiom and identity of an African people / Alamin M. Mazrui,
    Ibrahim Noor Shariff.
            p.   cm.
        Includes bibliographical references.
        ISBN 0-86543-310-0 (HB). -- ISBN 0-86543-311-9 (PBK).
        1. Swahili-speaking peoples. I. Shariff, Ibrahim Noor.
    II. Title.
    DT433.545.S93M39   1993
    305.896 ' 392--dc20   93-9903
                                                                    CIP

CONTENTS

*To the memory of
Shihabuddin Chiraghdin
and for
Bakari Shee Lali*

PREFACE

Writing about a particular people in a language that is foreign to them often poses a problem of choice between a terminology of authenticity and a terminology of intelligibility. With regard to Swahili studies, in particular, the tradition of terminological authenticity has sought to maintain a distinction between the following derivatives as used by the Swahili people themselves:

Kiswahili	=	Name of the language
Mswahili	=	Single member of the Swahili community
Waswahili	=	Swahili people
Uswahili	=	Swahili culture and ways of life
Uswahilini	=	Land inhabited by the Swahili

The tradition of terminological intelligibility, on the other hand, shows greater sensitivity to the linguistic rules of the medium of discourse itself, in this case the English language. The French people refer to their language as *Français*; but in English it is known as French. Intelligibility is likely to be affected if we were to retain the French term in an English sentence like "*Français* is spoken in over twenty African countries."

The same logic applies to "Swahili." Observing the different derivations of the term "Swahili" when writing in English would not be in accord with the morphological rules of the language. To do so, therefore, would be to maintain authenticity at the expense of intelligibility.

Many "Swahilists" are strong adherents of terminological authenticity and may consider a departure from this tradition as a kind of "terminological betrayal." In our opinion, however, both these traditions are equally valid. But because our readers may include those who are not familiar with the Swahili language, we have opted not to follow the common Swahilist terminological practice, in the interest of terminological intelligibility. Throughout this text, therefore, "Swahili" will appear independently without the usual prefixes and suffixes that distinguish between the language, the culture, the people, and their homeland.

In writing this book we owe a debt of gratitude to Dr. Ali A. Mazrui, our "elder statesman" of African Studies, and to Professors Aijaz Ahmad, Jaffer Kassim Ali, Omari Kokole, Nayla Orchardson-Mazrui, and Said S. Samatar, who read the typescript critically and made many invaluable suggestions. We owe a similar dept to Mary Benazzi and Dr. Jan Feidel. In addition to scholars, we owe debt to Safaa Muhammad Said-Shariff, who made the atmosphere in her home, where we did much of the writing, so affable and full of repose. To Darlene Smith, who typed the manuscript, often well past civilized working hours, we also owe a debt of gratitude.

INTRODUCTION

THE RELATIVITY OF IDENTITY

The Swahili are essentially a mixed people, the result of long crossing between the Negros of the coast and the Arabs, with an admixture of slave blood from nearly all the East African tribes. . . .
— *Encyclopaedia Britannica*, 1911

The Swahili is cheerful and happy-go-lucky as the African; fond of humour, intrigue and power as the Arab.
— *Captain Stigand*, 1913

. . . the Swahili [are] neither African nor Asian, but *sui generis*, an open society, tolerant and free.
— *Jan Knappert*, 1979

There is no such thing as Swahili tribe or group. . . .
— *Kenya Ministry of Tourism*

 above quotations constitute a small sample of views about the Swahili people that have been expressed over the years. These views are by no means atypical. The range of opinions is so wide, in fact, that an innocent reader of twentieth century writings on the Swahili people is bound to be left with a host of rather disturbing questions: Are the Swahili a community of Africanized Arabs? Arabized Africans? Or are they a peculiar combination of both? Are they genetically a "hybrid" people or merely socio-cultural "mutants"? Are they no more than a socio-linguistic unit of a sort, or do they constitute an ethnic

entity in some genetic sense of the word? Do they personify the domestication of Islam in Africa, or the dislocation of African spirituality? Are they the unique, honorable, and pioneering people of Shiva Naipaul's conception (189), or the split-image, "low, sordid, cunning, thieving, slanderous, callous and ignorant" superior animals of Captain Stigand's characterization (130)? In the sum of these views, Swahili identity emerges as profoundly enigmatic, creating a false impression that the people themselves are in the throes of an identity crisis.

To the modern research-oriented scholar, the scenario is so bewildering, in fact, that the verdict on Swahili identity is said to await further empirical investigation into the community and its psychological predisposition. Carol Eastman's proclamation after extensive and scientific survey of the subject is significant in this regard:

> The question "Who are the Waswahili?" is by no means answered here. Perhaps a more extensive study setting out to deal with this particular question which would consider various linguistic criteria as well as these attitudinal ones of "self" and "others" would be fruitful. (235)

No wonder, then, the Swahili community has become such a fertile terrain for aspiring "Africanists" from the northern hemisphere. As Shiva Naipaul observes with regard to the Swahili town of Lamu:

> It is impossible to be in Lamu for any length of time without encountering the professional researcher: Lamu has more researchers per head of population than doctors. Already I have met a German academic, a specialist in Swahili poetry, who was scouring the island in the hope of finding hitherto unpublished manuscripts; a photographer who was compiling a detailed visual record of the interiors of the finer Lamu houses; a sociologist who was studying the hapless descendants of fishermen who had migrated to Lamu from the Comoro Islands. Fecund island! There seemed no end to the dissertations to which it could give rise, the modest academic careers it could support.(185)

Naipaul makes these remarks following an anecdote in which he relates an encounter with two anthropologists who "have been resident in Lamu for some months collecting material for the theses they are writing. Carol is investigating divorce procedure; Dean is investigating the music played in the mosques" (185). Fecund Swahili island indeed!

The people referred to as the Swahili in this book occupy a narrow coastal strip of east Africa that stretches from Mozambique in the south, to Somalia in the north, and its adjacent islands. This area, which cuts across five African countries (Somalia, Kenya, Tanzania, Mozambique, and Comoro Islands), is also inhabited by other related peoples who have had a long history of symbiotic relationships with the Swahili. These peoples, collectively known as Mijikenda, together with the Swahili, to this day often use the term of mutual reference, *adzomba/wajomba* (maternal uncles), to symbolize the depth and extent of their relationship.

By virtue of its geography — its coastal location on the direct path of the monsoon winds, which blow seasonally from Asia to Africa and vice versa — this region became an intermediate zone of intercontinental trade between the peoples of the Arab world, of Persia, India, China, eastern and central Africa. This immense variety of people formed part of what came to be a flourishing Indian Ocean commercial and trade system that existed for centuries. The Swahili were thus centrally placed to become participants, and players, in a great socio-cultural and linguistic encounter, in a stadium of civilizations, with currents from several sources within and beyond Africa.

In the process, small communities of foreigners settled in the region, intermingled with and were absorbed into the local population. Consequently, under the influence of foreign settlers the indigenous population converted to Islam and Africanized the religion into local temper and taste. They fought among themselves along the lines of city-states and also fought in combination against foreign invaders. Treaties of protection were signed with some Arab nations, especially Oman. In the process they forged blood-brotherhood ties with some African people, such as the Kamba of Kenya; and, above all, a writing system emerged to document some of these events for posterity. The geography of the Swahili thus became the mother of their history, forging a civilization that is today recognized as one of the oldest in Africa, a civilization that has served with others to demonstrate the richness and genius of Africa's heritage.

The Swahili people thus entered the twentieth century with (1) an ancient tradition that no study of the history of Africa can ignore; (2) a centuries-old writing tradition that has further promoted the collective consciousness of the Swahili people and that has served to shed light on their history and civilization; and (3) a visible homogeneity of culture cemented by an Islamic ethos. With such a background, one would have thought that the *identity* of the Swahili people would never be a matter of debate nor an issue that might unsettle the tranquility of any informed mind. Yet, twentieth century writings about this group of people are replete with misconceptions and distortions about their identity, culture, language, and literature to the point where relentless debates on "Who are the Swahili?" have become legion.

In the following pages we shall attempt to demonstrate that this seeming muddle as to the definition of a Swahili is not intrinsic to Swahili identity; it is, rather, a problem that is fused into the tinted glasses of Eurocentricity,[1] through which the Swahili have been viewed over the years. The kinds of questions posed, the presuppositions made, the set of axioms posited, and the very methodological approaches adopted in the study of the subject betray the "Africanist" bias, and sometimes arrogance, of Eurocentricity. The cumulative result of this imposed paradigm has been a people dispossessed of their identity, their history and, to some degree, their political and economic rights.

Are these misconceptions about the Swahili merely products of innocent scholarly pursuits in the context of certain socio-historical coincidences, or are they predicated upon motives that have deep political foundations? It is quite understandable that the Swahili people would attract the intellectual curiosity of a newcomer from the northern hemisphere: after all, the Swahili do have certain socio-historical peculiarities that have engendered their sense of identity and destiny over time. But what may have begun as a passing "appreciation" of the dimensions of human composition and experience soon turned into a scholarly fixation bound by the politics of the time. Even the seemingly innocent scholarly publications were now contributing to the legitimating ideologies of the different interest groups that have a stake in the identity of the Swahili people. Swahili identity thus became increasingly interwoven into the complex disarray of east African politics, and it has become impossible to talk of Swahili identity in terms that are neutral and nonpartisan.

But the identity of any people is in fact never neutral. The concept of identity that defines "the self" and "the other," "the we" and "the they," is always rooted in the politics of its time and place. Identity is, in fact, a process by which power and status are negotiated, disinheritance and oppression legitimized, and liberation struggles waged. Intellectual debates on the identity of a particular people, therefore, are seldom free of political underpinnings revolving around struggles of dominance and liberation, of subjection and autonomy.

It was certainly not the innocent pen of history that dubbed the Boers more African (Afrikaners) than the Africans (Kaffir/Bantu), or made the European invaders of the "new world" the "real" Americans while its native population came to be known merely as "Indian," or dispossessed the African population of every attribute of its being except its color. Nor is the quest for redefinition among African peoples of the Diaspora or natives of the Americas intended to satisfy the intellectual whims of these populations. These intellectual instances of definition, counter-definition, and redefinition, the changing nature of ethnicity in various parts of Africa, the clashes for ethnic autonomy in what was once the Soviet Union, all revolve around the concept of identity as shaped specifically by the vissicitudes of the politics and economics of time and place. In other words, identity is both *relative* and *dynamic*. It is given a different substance by different interest groups and assumes a different form under different politico-economic circumstances. As Joel Samoff once perceptively put it, "All people have multiple identities — which identity is salient depends on the situation" (19).

There is probably no term that best captures the relativism and dynamism of identity than the Swahili word *kabila*. Unfortunately, the tendency to predicate the dynamics of African societies on the anthropological category "tribe" has led many people to regard the Swahili *kabila* as the equivalent

5

of the English word "tribe" (or ethnic group).[2] But, in fact, *kabila* has neither the semantic narrowness, nor the negativeness, in its connotation, of the English term "tribe." Depending on who is talking to whom, and the particular circumstances in which they are "interlocuting," a question like "What is your *kabila*?" may appropriately evoke any of the following responses that reflect different levels of consciousness of being: "Shikeli" (a member of the Shikeli "clan" — an intra-Swahili genetic consciousness), "Muamu" (a native of Lamu Island — an intra-Swahili-geographical consciousness), "Swahili" (a pan-Swahili cultural consciousness), "Mwislamu" (a Muslim — an extra-Swahili religious consciousness), "Mkenya" (a Kenyan — an extra-Swahili national consciousness), "Mwafrika" (an African — an extra-Swahili pan-African consciousness), or "Mwarabu" (an Arab — a transcontinental "genetic" consciousness).

In terms of understanding the present debate on the definition of the Swahili, however, the relativity of identity is best seen in terms of the varied "criteria" used by different peoples who have come into contact with the Swahili to "define" who is and who is not a member of the "inner-group." It is hoped that this will lead to a better appreciation of the contribution of alien paradigms of identity in the creation of the present muddle about Swahili identity in particular and about the identity of several other African nationalities in general. As we turn to a discussion of some of these paradigms, however, we would like to caution the reader that these are merely abstractions that are not unsusceptible to qualifications across time and space.

The Afrocentric Paradigm

The Afrocentric paradigm is an abstraction based on societies indigenous to the African continent, especially prior to the inception of European colonial rule. Such societies ranged from speakers of Khoisan languages in southern Africa to those of Semitic languages (like Amharic, Arabic, Gurage, etc.) in the northern part of the continent; and from speakers of Nilotic languages in eastern Africa to those of Kwa languages in western Africa. In essence, then, it is an abstraction emerging from an extensive multicultural base. And to describe this paradigm we would like to begin with a myth on the origins of the Gikuyu people of Kenya.

In his celebrated book *Facing Mount Kenya*, Jomo Kenyatta, the first president of Kenya, gives a narrative account of the origins of the Gikuyu that, though mythical in the sense that there is less than sufficient evidence of authenticity, has served as an important historical-symbolic source of Gikuyu identity. We are informed in this narrative that "Mogai" (the diviner of the universe) once called Gikuyu (the founder-to-be of the Gikuyu nationality) and gave him his share of land. At the allocated spot Gikuyu found a beautiful woman named Moombi with whom he had nine *daughters* but no sons. Kenyatta writes:

> Gikuyu was very disturbed at not having a male heir. In his despair, he called upon Mogai to advise him on the situation. He responded quickly and told Gikuyu not to be perturbed, but to have patience and everything would be done according to his wish. . .
>
> Gikuyu did as he was directed by the Mogai or Ngai, and so it happened that when he returned to the sacred tree, there he found the promised nine young men who greeted him warmly. . .
>
> Gikuyu told the young men that if they wished to marry his daughters he would give his consent only if they agree to live in his homestead under a matriarchal system.
>
> The young men agreed to his condition, and after a short time all of them were married, and soon established their own family sets. . . . (6-7)

The Gikuyu thus came into being as a distinct *kabila* with nine internal divisions (*mbari*) seen to have a common bond despite the fact that their paternal origins were unknown. And it has remained to this day that a matrilineal descent, combined with the acquisition of Gikuyu culture and the Gikuyu language as a mother tongue, are the parameters within which Gikuyu identity is situated. Similar parameters of identity can be seen in operation in many other African societies. The line of descent is combined with cultural and linguistic attributes to provide a people with their distinct stamp of identity.

In many cases, in fact, in the absence of an identifiable line of descent, the linguistic and cultural features alone are sufficient to place a person within a particular group. There is abundant literature today that attests to the flexible nature of ethnicity in Africa, whereby, on the basis of cultural and linguistic considerations, individuals acquire "shifting," multiple identities, moving in and out of different ethnic groups, as the politics and economics of the place demand. It is precisely these dynamics in the African situation that would make a question like "Are you a Hausa?" answerable in the affirmative or negative by the same individual, depending on who asks the question, the circumstances under which the question is asked, the assumptions behind the question, and so forth.

As intimated earlier, the Swahili are not different in this regard. They recognize a geographical contiguity, a quasigenetic historicity and a cultural commonality that, in their consciousness, easily define their collective identity. They recognize internal divisions within the community in terms of linguistic-cum-geographical units, each of which is in turn divided into clear units. In Kenya, for example, the following Swahili geolinguistic units are said to exist:

Group	Dialect
Watikuu/Wabajuni	Kitikuu/Kibajuni
Wapate	Kipate
Wasiu	Kisiu
Waamu	Kiamu
Wamvita	Kimvita
Wajomvu	Kijomvu
Wavumba	Kivumba
Wachifundi	Chichifundi

Each of the above groups can be further subdivided into clans and lineages. These would include: Wayumbili pembe, Wayumbili ng'ombe, Wayumbe, Wafamau and Wakinamte, among the *Waamu*; or the Wang'andu, Watutu, Wakande, Wafamau, Muongo Bakari and Wana wa Ndege, among the *Wapate*, and so forth.

Of course, not all people categorized as Swahili today would fit into the social schema described above. Because of intermarriage, and owing to diverse cultural, religious, and linguistic factors, people of other African, Arab, Persian, and Indian origin were continuously absorbed into Swahili society, participating in the total life of its community, contributing to its reproduction in diverse and complex ways without destroying its internal fabric. Paternal descendants of the Swahili automatically became Swahili irrespective of their national origins, and non-Swahili settlers of various African and non-African origins became fully acculturated into a Swahili identity without losing their "otherness" in the process.

Through the parameters of descent (matrilineal and patrilineal), behavioral, cultural, and linguistic assimilation, therefore, many an African community may be said to veer towards a notion of identity that is assimilative and flexible, towards a concept of belonging that is truly liberal. As we shall attempt to demonstrate later on, however, this African liberalism, in matters of identity, has been of mixed blessing to the Swahili people. It has been both an asset and a liability in the changing politics of the east African region.

The Arabocentric Paradigm

Arabocentricity can be defined as the paradigm characteristic of the Arab people spread between parts of Africa and the Arabian Peninsula.[3] There is a sense, then, in which the Arabocentric paradigm is merely a subset of the Afrocentric paradigm, and, as expected, it is in conformity with the "Afrocentric norm."

Like the Swahili and many other African peoples, the Arabs have a concept of identity that is accommodating and liberal. Those who are today known as the Arab people can at least trace some aspects of their history to the Arabian Peninsula, even though relatively few Arabs can be said to be of Arabian origin. The overwhelming majority of Arabs originate from regions other than Arabia and not too long ago spoke languages other than Arabic. They are a people who, in a sense, became "Arabized." Over seventy percent of "Arab lands" are in Africa, and many of the people therein are indigenous to the African continent. The tendency of Arab identity to absorb ultimately led to the emergence of a cohesive group of people with a wide range of skin pigmentation. Ali Mazrui comments in this regard:

> In skin color the range is from the white Arabs of Syria and Lebanon, the brown Arabs of Hadhramout and the Yemen, to the black Arabs of parts of Saudi Arabia, Oman and, of course, the Sudan. If the father is Arab, the offspring is Arab without qualification . . . the idea of a half-caste being virtually alien to the relational universe of this mongrel race. (1964:22)

But as intimated above, it is not only paternal ancestry that qualifies one for Arab identity. There is also the phenomenon of linguistic assimilation: Anyone to whom Arabic is a first language is almost automatically an Arab regardless of his/her "national" or "racial" origins. In addition to the wide range of colors, therefore, Arab identity is also marked by a vast multiplicity of "national" or "racial" origins. As Erskine Childers puts it:

> The Arab world . . . comprises very many widely varying races or historical groups. The short list is bewildering, and distinguishing racial definitions are themselves treacherous. From west to east, the list must include Berbers, Carthaginians, Romans, Vandals, Arabians, Turkomans, Egyptians, Nubians, Haemites, Greeks, Armenians, Circassians, Assyrians, Babilonians, Hittites, Sumarians, Kurds, Persians, and a small host of ancient migratory infusions whom it is safer to describe simply as Semitic. (17)

Indeed the Arabs have demonstrated a degree of openness towards their identity, a degree of communal accommodativeness, that goes even beyond that of the Swahili. In the Swahili people's own definition of the term Swahili, the faith of Islam still seems to feature as an important criterion. And even though there are definite dynamics in east African geopolitics that have begun to challenge the Islamic factor in Swahili identity, one would not be altogether wrong to claim that Swahili identity necessarily includes an Islamic component even today. This is certainly not the case with Arab identity. Arab identity traverses all "barriers" except the linguistic one. So inasmuch as "Arabness" cuts across "national/racial" lines, it also transcends boundaries of a religious nature. In religious affiliation Arabs include Muslims, Jews, and Christians as well as people who belong to other religions.

The Eurocentric Paradigm

What is noticeable in both the Afrocentric and Arabocentric paradigms is the almost complete disregard of skin color as a qualifying feature of identity. This ceases to be the case when we begin to consider northern paradigms of identity that, at a certain level, treat "color" as an indispensable ingredient of identity, an essential marker of what constitutes an in-group and an out-group. This does not mean, of course, that Africans and Arabs were or are "color blind." But the color consciousness found among Africans and Arabs has been of a kind that *does not* preclude others from acquiring a particular African or Arab identity. Nor can it be said here that peoples of the northern hemisphere were oblivious to features of identity other than color. Genealogical, cultural, and linguistic considerations also come into play in Eurocentric notions of identity. But unlike their African and Arab counterparts, color became central in the conception of the northern man. Color automatically limits the inclusiveness of northern identity, be it Germanic, Latin, or Slavonic.

Nonetheless, the northerners themselves have not been in unison with regard to the use of skin color in setting the limits of identity. Their difference, however, has essentially been one of emphasis. As we shall discuss later, there has been greater emphasis on color as a feature of identity among the Germanic than among the Latin people. Perhaps partly because of the longer history of exposure to peoples of color from the African side of the Mediterranean, Latin nations have tended to show greater tolerance for color differences. Greater familiarity in this instance may have engendered greater tolerance. In contrast to their Germanic counterparts, therefore, the Latin people have sometimes placed greater weight on linguistic-cultural attributes of identity than on pigmentational ones. Even in their racism towards other people, therefore, the Latin people have tended to be more cultural bigots than color racists. In Program

9 of his television series *The Africans: A Triple Heritage,* Ali Mazrui elaborates:

> The French seem to believe that culture flows through the veins of society the way blood flows through the arteries of the human body; that culture is to society what blood is to the human person. Well, it is a measure of how seriously they take culture in human affairs and how this has influenced interracial relations. They say the French don't care who goes to bed with whom provided the preliminaries are conducted in impeccable French. Well, it is a distinction between color prejudice and culture prejudice. In cultural discrimination, there is no doubt that the French are worse offenders than the British. In color prejudice, it is the British that are the worse offenders.

It is precisely this greater emphasis on language and culture, generally, that informed the assimilationist policies of the Latin colonizers of Africa. The Italians, the French, the Portuguese, and the Spanish became slightly more accommodating to colonial subjects who became linguistically and culturally assimilated. The Germanic people, on the other hand, have tended to place greater emphasis on color than Latin people.

But on the question of European identity, specifically, Latin and Germanic differences are essentially neutralized. Neither a single European parentage, nor any amount of cultural and linguistic assimilation, nor a combination of both these factors, would earn a person, with even the remotest African ancestral connections, for example, a German or English or French identity. Double "white" parentage that can ensure a "pure" whiteness of skin color is indispensable in qualifying for European identity. This explains why after more than 400 years of uninterrupted residence in America and Britain, speaking English as the first and only language, and producing racially mixed offsprings, the so-called "black" man in these countries has not been accepted into the mainstream. In America he has remained a "Negro," a "black," or "American" with some qualification; similarly, in England he may be a British citizen but not English.

Ali Mazrui described the contrast between the Eurocentric and non-Eurocentric paradigms of identity in the following hypothetical terms:

. . . If the white citizens of the United States had, in fact, been Arab, most of the colonized citizens would have become Arab too. It has been estimated that over seventy percent of the Negro population in the United States has some "white" blood. And the "white" blood was much more often than not derived from a white father. Now given the "principle" that if the father is Arab the child is Arab, most of the Negroes of the United States would have been Arab had the white people of the United States been Arab too. But the white Americans are Caucasian and the dominant culture is Germanic. And so if either of the parent is non-Germanic, the offspring cannot be Germanic either. (1964:22)

Mazrui's statement is, of course, quite ahistorical, but it helps in *dramatizing* the differences in some of the paradigms of identity that exist today. And Mazrui may well have added that if the white people of the United States were Arab, and the English language were Arabic, the entire African-American population would have been Arab simply by virtue of their linguistic assimilation. But, in the relational universe of the European people, linguistic and cultural assimilation rank well below dual European parentage as a determinant of European identity.

To recapitulate, then, we have attempted to demonstrate the relativity inherent in the concept of identity by giving concrete examples of criteria used by different people to determine who is and who is not one of their own kind. This relativity, however, is not static. It may assume different forms in different circumstances. We are used to thinking of Europeans as being "racially" exclusive in relation to members of other "races." But, in fact, under certain politico-economic circumstances, one group of Europeans may manifest attitudes towards another group of Europeans that border on "racism." The same may apply to people of Asian, African, and other origins. Therefore, what we call "racism" may, in fact, be "interracial" or "intra-racial." It may be expressed in different ways and with different degrees of crudeness under different sets of circumstances. In short, criteria of identity of "self" and "other" are constantly being redefined on the basis of politico-economic equations.

In addition, the paradigms of identity outlined above are not only subject to vagaries of a politico-economic nature, but also have an important historical dimension to them. This historicity is rooted in the politics of power. Exclusivist notions of identity, for example, are more likely to emerge among a people who have the material might to subjugate others than among those who do not possess such material power; among the powerless, on the other hand, an identitarian consciousness may emerge as a diffusive reflex against the bigotry of the powerful. The awareness that a "nation" has the power to conquer and dominate others tends to lead to a conception of identity of the "self" that more rigidly seeks to exclude the "others." What we have termed Afrocentric, Arabocentric, and Eurocentric paradigms of identity, then, are in a sense historical expressions of the development of material forces on a global scale.

Prior to the inception of European colonial rule in Africa, most African societies had precapitalist, communal economies that engendered no more than a subsistence standard of living.[4] Such economies did not allow for a degree of surplus accumulation that could empower the society to overcome its own insecurities, let alone to conquer and maintain dominance over other people for any significant length of time. In inter-ethnic confrontations the number of combatants was often more decisive than technological might. The security and longevity of African societies under communal economic systems was often not unrelated to sheer demographic factors. An exclusivist concept of the "self" under these circumstances, therefore, could have threatened the very survival of a people. This is the general politico-economic context from which the liberalism of the Afrocentric paradigm of identity emerged.

The Arabocentric concept of identity, on the other hand, may have arisen out of what Samir Amin (1989) calls a tributary mode of production that began in antiquity and stretched well into the European Renaissance period. Though precapitalist, these medieval societies did engage in sufficient accumulation to develop a material power base for the conquest and subjugation of other societies. At no time, however, was this material power strong enough to guarantee long-term and pervasive dominance over others. For example, Krapf (1968) describes how Arab and African "subjects" submitted to the "nominal pretensions" of the Sultan of Oman as long as "their own arrangements are not too stringently interfered with. They receive the Sultan's governors and pay the dues which he levies from their ports; but beyond that Said [sic] Said seems to have no hope of their obedience and subjection" (124).

In many cases, then, lacking adequate material power, functionaries of medieval rulers had to assimilate into the societies they ruled in order to maintain some semblance of hegemony over any substantial period of time. Medieval rulers had to be one with the people, and the people one with them, to survive as rulers. Arab rulers of the Swahili coast, for example, had to "Swahilize," and allow the Swahili socio-cultural space to "Arabize," if Arab rule was to have any chance of continuation. The inclusiveness and liberalism of Arab identity, therefore, evolved from this medieval politico-economic crucible.

Throughout the medieval period, Europe itself belonged to a regional tributary system that included Europeans and Arabs, Christians and Muslims. The greater part of Europe, however, was located at the periphery of this system. Its center was Latin Europe located around the Mediterranean basin. It is in this center of the European tributary system that early forms of capitalism began to emerge. The degree and forms of accumulation engendered by the capitalist mode of production led to a tremendous concentration of material power. One of the central components of the legitimating ideology of this emergent capitalism was its materialism and racism, which, according to Amin, became "the fundamental basis on which European cultural unity was constructed" (90). From the Renaissance onwards, however, the center of the world capitalist system shifted towards the shores of the Atlantic, while Mediterranean Europe became relegated to the periphery. European culture then reconstructed itself around an ideological myth that created an opposition between an alleged European geographical and cultural continuity and the world south of the Mediterranean. "The whole of Eurocentricism," according to Amin, "lies in this mythic construct" (11). It is at this point that Europe became conscious of its power, and its conquest of the world became a realizable objective. It is around this possibility that racist notions of identity of "self" and "others" began to crystallize in

Europe, especially in Germanic Europe, which had become the center of world capitalism.[5]

What we have attempted to do, then, is to give a sketch of the historical forces that lie behind the relativity of some of the paradigms of identity described above. With this background in mind, we shall try to demonstrate in Chapter One how the confusion over Swahili identity was prompted by the relative vantage points of different interest groups and the changing politico-economic circumstances of the east African region. This relativity was both external (i.e., how the Swahili were viewed by different people at different points in time) as well as internal (i.e., how different Swahili people emphasized different aspects of their identity at different points in time). This part of our argument adopts a historical approach beginning with the oldest available records of the Swahili coast.

The "confusion" over Swahili identity has also been intertwined with distorted views about the Swahili language. These will form the subject matter of Chapter Two. Chapters Three and Four deal specifically with the literary dimension of the issue, and with how questions of Swahili literary form, literary history and literary interpretation have contributed to the problem of identity. In the Epilogue, we shall examine some of the political implications of this apparent confusion about Swahili identity.

PART ONE
ETHNICITY, LANGUAGE, AND IDENTITY

CHAPTER ONE:
SWAHILI IDENTITY REVISITED

 are the Swahili? This question has often prompted a quest for "origins," a search for that historical moment at which, as well as the historical process by which, the Swahili people can be said to have come into being. The problem of identity and the quest for origins in the particular manner applied to the Swahili case is not a very usual scholarly engagement compared to the way it has occurred with other African nationalities. Perhaps the strength of oral traditions that perpetuate myths of common ancestors among these other nationalities have given their identities an appearance of historicity that seem to render the issue of their origins less problematic. But in the case of the Swahili, the evolution of the written word centuries before European colonization, as well as the Islamic doctrine that came with its own version of the origins of human beings and their variation, may have undermined the substance and potency of Swahili oral traditions in the historical consciousness of the people.

Whatever the case, the remaining sprinklings of myths and legends, found, for example, in *vave* songs that deal with the origins of some Swahili groups, have not been very helpful in convincing "Swahilists" that the Swahili people may, in fact, have a sense of a common historical past and destiny. As a result, the search for Swahili origins has continued to be featured quite prominently in the scholarly agendas of Swahilists of various shades. And most of the approaches in the course of this search have tended to be overwhelmingly atomistic, ignoring the wider historical picture within which the Swahili coast has been situated during approximately the last two thousand years. It is for this reason that we decided to tackle this question of Swahili identity from a historical point of view, our objective being to show how the superimposition of alien notions of identity forged by external historical circumstances, under certain conditions of local historical developments, may have contributed to confounding the question of Swahili identity. And it is to this discussion that we must now turn.

The earliest known document that gives us an inkling of the people who may have inhabited the east African coast as early as the beginning of the Christian era is *The Periplus of the Erythrean Sea*, which has been translated into English from the Greek original by Freeman-Grenville. While the author is unknown, and the work is deemed to have been written in the first century, the revelant passage from this document states:

> Men of the greatest stature, who are pirates, inhabit the whole coast and at each place have set up chiefs. The chief of the Ma'afir is the Suzerain, according to an ancient right which subordinates it to the kingdom which has become the first in Arabia. The people of Mouza hold it in tribute under his sovereignty and send there small ships, mostly with Arab captains and crew who trade and intermarry with mainlanders of all the places and know their language. (2)

Several issues that have direct bearing on the present debate about Swahili identity seem to emerge clearly from this quotation, assuming, in fact, that it does refer to the Swahili coast as many historians seem inclined to believe:

1. First, there is the assumption that the region had a population of "indigenes" that was clearly non-Arabian.[6]

2. These "indigenes" were nonetheless under the administrative authority of some Arabian suzerain. It is possible that this administrative arrangement was what in modern parlance might be called "colonial." But it is also possible that just as Egypt, in all its "African blackness" (as argued by Cheikh Anta

Diop), once belonged to a Mediterranean civilization and only later became African in the political geography of our time, the Swahili coast, at this juncture, may have belonged to a "Red Sea civilization" that only later metamorphosed into a separate social organism.

3. Furthermore, Arabians had long and extensive trade contacts with these east African coastal people and intermarriage between these Arabians and locals was already a growing reality. This process of intermarriage, which seemed so organic to the writer of the *Periplus* that he accorded it no more than a passing remark, came to haunt the minds of racists and Eurocentrists almost two thousand years later.

4. Finally, the document also presupposes that the people along the entire east African coast had one *common* language, a language different from Arabic, which, nonetheless, because of economic, social, and marital ties, the Arabians came to comprehend and presumably speak in communicating with the indigenous people.

The *Periplus* does not, of course, identify these coastal people as specifically Swahili. But it is possible to make this deduction from what obtains today. First, piracy presumes a maritime culture. Of all the peoples inhabiting the east coast of Africa, the Swahili continue to be the only group that looks to the sea for its livelihood. Virtually all the other coastal nationalities have land-based economic activities, be it hunting, gathering, or farming. In addition, according to Said Samatar, the piratic feats of the Swahili are to this day well known in parts of Somalia, especially among the urban Benaadiris, who still speak with disdain of the "sea-prowling" Swahili (1989:8).

Second, the Swahili today are a living expression of an African-Arab process of intermarriage which may have started even prior to the Christian era. No other community along the entire east African coast could claim a comparable degree of marital interaction with Arabs to warrant the observation made in the *Periplus* almost two thousand years ago.

Finally, as intimated earlier and consonant with the description in the *Periplus*, Swahili is the only language in that entire region that is spoken along the whole of this coast-line, from the southern coast of Somalia to the northern coast of Mozambique. All the other coastal languages are more localized, even though current economic processes have prompted a population flux that may ultimately alter this linguistic equation.

In short, then, the prevailing scenario on the east coast of Africa has several important characteristics that bear a close resemblance to some aspects of the picture drawn in the *Periplus*. In view of these historical parallels, separated by a period of almost two thousand years, one would not be wrong to suggest that the "piratic people of great stature" described in the *Periplus* were, in fact, the Swahili in formation — whether or not they used that particular term to define themselves.

For the next eight hundred years or so after the anonymous Greek traveller who authored the *Periplus*, we see virtually no other documentation that would shed some light on the people of the east African coast during this early period. The next most important documentary phase concerning the east African coastal dwellers, then, is that of Arab travellers. One of the earliest Arab accounts of the Swahili coast is probably that of Al-Mas'udi, written during the first half of the tenth century. In this account Al-Mas'udi describes the population of the coast as religiously mixed, with Muslims and what he calls "idolaters." For the first time, then, we get a glimpse of what may have been a pre-Islamic Swahili population. According to Al-Mas'udi, "one of their holy men will often gather a crowd and exhort his hearers to please God in their lives and to be obedient to Him. He explains the punishments that follow upon disobedience, and reminds them of their ancestors and kings of old. These people have no religious law; their kings rule by custom and political expediency." Al-Mas'udi also added that the Zanj have kings known as *Wafalme* (a Swahili word current to this day), and that they have an elegant language and men who preach in it (Freeman-Grenville, 16).

The Greek writer of the *Periplus* visited the east African coast in the pre-Islamic period; naturally, therefore, he had nothing to say about the presence of this religion at that time. But within three hundred years of the emergence of Islam in Arabia, Al-Mas'udi could already inform us of the existence of a substantial Muslim population on the east African coast. This further confirms the observations made in the *Periplus* that there was extensive and long interaction between the peoples on both sides of the Persian/Arabian Gulf.

Again Al-Mas'udi, himself an Arab, did not regard the Zanj people as Arabs or of Arab origin. He regarded them as people different from the Arabs with their own language, which, to his foreign ears, sounded rather elegant. If there were "Arab settlers," they were probably already assimilated, otherwise Al-Mas'udi would definitely have mentioned a familiar Arab element in an alien environment. And if there was a mixed range of skin colors, as there was bound to be, given the long history of African-Arab intermarriage, it did not strike him as odd or worthy of any specific mention. Whatever their color combinations, whatever the differences in their religious persuasion, the perceived commonality in their elegant tongue was sufficient, it seems, to make Al-Mas'udi regard these as one people, the Zanj people.

Al-Idrisi, writing in the twelfth century, and basing his work on accounts of other writers and informants, also presents a view of the people of the east African coast that is in conformity with the Arab paradigm of identity. At this point there is little doubt that Al-Idrisi is talking about a Swahili-speaking people who identified five kinds of bananas (i.e., *kundi, fili, omani, muriani,* and *sukari*) — all obviously Swahili words — as their staple food, complemented by fish, meat, and rice. He again notes, specifically citing Zanzibar, that the inhabitants are religiously mixed though, by this time, predominantly Muslim (Freeman-Grenville, 19-20).

Equally relevant to our discussion is Al-Idrisi's description of the people of "Djawaga islands" and their relationship to the inhabitants of Zanzibar. "Djawagans," according to Al-Idrisi, "are very dark in color" and travel "to Zanzibar in large and small ships, and use them for trading their goods, for they understand each other's language." Whether we take Djawaga islands to mean the islands of the Lamu Archipelago or, less likely, those of the Comoros, Al-Idrisi's description suggests that they and the people of Zanzibar may have spoken varieties of a common language, most probably Swahili. On that basis, therefore, they are likely to have shared a common sense of their identity. Be that as it may, Al-Idrisi, like Al-Mas'udi before him, while noting a color and a religious variation among the inhabitants of the east African coast, was not led to question their collective identity. He seems to have regarded them as

21

one people, the Zanj.

As a final example of the Arab perception of the people of the east African coast let us consider Ibn Battuta, the Arab traveller who lived, travelled extensively, and wrote in the fourteenth century. Ibn Battuta refers specifically to his trip to "the land of the Swahili," possibly the Lamu area, and to the town of Kilwa, that "most beautiful and well-constructed town in the world" with roofs built with mangrove poles. The people of Kilwa are described as Zanj, of very black complexion with distinctive facial marks. The townspeople at this stage are primarily Muslim but live side by side with their "pagan" brethren with whom they are engaged in a "holy war." At the same time, Arab religious notables from the Hijaz, Iraq, and other Arab countries used to come to Kilwa to visit its King, who is described as humble and charitable (Freeman-Grenville, 31).

Again despite the color differences that Ibn Battuta noticed in the land of Zanj, and despite the differences in religion that seem to have erupted into a "jihad" of a sort between "brothers," Ibn Battuta was not unconscious of the unity of identity of these people. Some may have been Swahili, some unspecified, some Muslims, some "pagans," some light and some dark, but all were subsumed under a common Zanj identity.

Following in the footsteps of the Arabs were Portuguese travellers to the east coast of Africa. Portugal, as part of the Iberian peninsula, belonged to the Mediterranean wing of Europe. This region, as suggested in the introduction, served as the center of European tributary and, later, the periphery of European capitalist systems. By the time the Portuguese visited east Africa, they were a leading force of mercantile capitalism, using both Christianity (i.e., religious differences) and racism (i.e., differences of culture and color) as their ideological justification. This ideology is clearly reflected in a bull of Pope Nicholas V granting the King of Portugal the monopoly of trade with African peoples, provided they were brought willingly or by force to baptism. The bull stated:

> We, after scrupulous reflection, are granting by our Bull full and entire freedom to King Alphonso to conquer, to besiege, to fight, and to submit all the Saracens, Pagans, and other enemies of Christ, wherever they may be; and to seize

the kingdoms, the dukedoms, the princedoms, the lord-ships, personal properties, landed properties, and all the wealth they withhold and possess; and to submit these persons to a perpetual slavery; to appropriate these kingdoms, duchies, principalities, counties, lordships, properties and wealth; to transmit them to their successors; to take advantage and make use of them personally and with their offspring. As they have received the so-called powers, King Alphonso and the Infanta have acquired, possess, and will possess, rightly and indefinitely, these islands, seas, and this wealth. . . . (Kesteloot, 86)

A religious and cultural racism thus became the cornerstone for the massacre, enslavement, and dispossession of entire peoples.

It is through the tinted lenses of this aspect of the Eurocentric paradigm that the Portuguese came to see the people they encountered on the shores of east Africa. If the Arabs before them perceived the people of the east coast of Africa as a distinct group, their Islamic faith notwithstanding, this distinctiveness was simply invisible to the Portuguese. They saw no difference between Muslims, whom they called Moors, and Arabs. The Swahili people were now simply subsumed under a more general, transcontinental category of "Moors," and their culture was nothing but "Moorish" in the eyes of the Portuguese. The variation in color did not, of course, go unnoticed: There were some "white Moors," some "tawny Moors," and some "black Moors." "But Moors the Swahili remained in the eyes of the Portuguese" (Chiraghdin, 1966: 2). The French also are known to have referred to the Muslim Swahili as "Moors" and distinguished them from "Arabs" and (non-Muslim) Africans (Nicholls, 1971: 24).

Using this religious-cum-racist ideology as a veneer for their mercantilist designs, the Portuguese subjected the Swahili people to some of the most heinous brutalities ever experienced in the history of east Africa. It was like a repeat of the Crusades, but on a smaller scale. In his celebrated television documentary *Africa*, Basil Davidson narrates:

In the year 1498 an event took place which was to lead, not only to the ruin of Kilwa, but in due course, to the destruction of Swahili trading network all along the coast. In that year, for the first time in history, three small Portuguese ships under the command of Vasco da Gama sailed round the Cape of Good Hope and into the Indian Ocean. The European incursion had begun. Returning home Vasco da Gama reported what he had seen and just seven years later a much larger and more menacing fleet appeared on the horizon. A German eyewitness called Hans Mayr has left an account of what took place: Admiral d'Almeida came here with fourteen men-of-war and six caravels. He ordered the ships to have their artillery ready. At dawn on Thursday the 24th of July all went into their boats to the shore. They went straight to the palace and only those inhabitants who did not resist were granted their lives. At the palace the Holy Cross was put down and Admiral d'Almeida prayed, then everyone started to plunder the town of all its merchandise.

Further north, Mombasa showed a militant resistance and the Portuguese unleashed their wrath. Adds Coupland:

> Finally the town was set on fire at several points, and a strong wind aiding, was thoroughly burnt out. When the Portuguese had gone and the people of Mombasa crept back to their gutted out and blackened town, they found, wrote the Sheikh to his fellow ruler at Malindi, "no living thing in it, neither man nor woman, young or old, nor child, however little: all who failed to make their escape had been killed or burnt." (45)

Other Swahili towns met with similar fate; with regard to the Swahili town of Faza, for example, "[t]he Portuguese not only sacked it," writes Davidson, "but are said to have killed every living thing they found, men, women, and children, even down to the household dogs and parrots"(1969:115). "Bursting through gray ocean doors upon this brilliant scene," adds Davidson, "the Portuguese almost at once began to loot and burn. They broke into city after city, sacking and stealing" (1991:193).

The brutality of the Portuguese and their attempted colonial invasion of Swahililand, justified on the basis of a racist-cum-religious ideology, was met with militant resistance at various points. If it is at all a blessing that at least parts of what is today Kenya and Tanzania did not follow the destiny of Mozambique, the credit goes to the resistance of the Swahili and their supporters,[7] which made it impossible for Portuguese rule to take root in that region of east Africa. But despite the brutality of the Portuguese, their racism at the conceptual level did not encroach completely on the sphere of skin color and "racial genetics." It revolved substantially around the cultural domain. It was primarily a cultural racism that, nonetheless, contributed in no small measure in obfuscating Swahili identity, by associating the Swahili with Arabs under the Islamic, i.e., "Moorish," umbrella. It failed to distinguish between religious identity and ethnic identity. Thus the wide range of colors among the Swahili did not seem to have become a substantial issue until after their encounter with Germanic Europeans.

The arrival of people of Germanic origin on the east coast of Africa suddenly put the issue of Swahili skin pigmentation on the agenda of Swahili identity against the background of the racial genetics of the time. But even in this case it was not until the nineteenth century, when the forces of capitalism had already taken deep root in Europe, and its subsequent ideology of European racial superiority had been thoroughly ingrained in the minds of its people, that skin color came to be featured in European scholarship on the Swahili people.[8]

One of the earliest nineteenth century European visitors to the east coast of Africa was James Prior, who published an account of his voyages, *Voyage of the Nisus Frigate*, in 1819. Commenting on the demographic composition of the Swahili coast, Prior states, "The people are descendants of the Arabs, who penetrated along the whole eastern coast as far as Cape Corrientes at an early period. . . . At present the natives bear the same features of face, but without the least portion of that energy of character by which their ancestors were distinguished" (Freeman-Grenville, 205-06). What had hitherto been an organic "duality" of the Swahili heritage was now split asunder, its Africanity isolated and considered responsible for the people's lack of that energy of character associated with Arabness. "African blood" was thus deemed too potent (or too poisonous) to allow any positive elements of a genetically defined Arabness to be encoded into the DNA of the Swahili. The Africanity of the Swahili, therefore, became a liability, depriving them of the redeeming characteristics that they may otherwise have gained from their supposed Arab ancestry.

Further on, commenting on the Swahili of Kilwa specifically, Prior writes:

> The people are generally good figures, being tall and well-made, and possessing regular and expressive features; the mere animal is fine, but its mind requires strict discipline and cultivation to be of use. The character seems indolent, not so amiable as that of the Johannese, and without any portion of that warlike energy and independence of feeling for which the Arabs have been famed. . . . They profess Mahometism, but do not very strictly adhere to it. (Freeman-Grenville, 210-11)

Here we see how the Eurocentric paradigm of identity begins to be used as an *a priori* justification for colonialism. Identity is now placed on a vertical plane in terms of an assumed hierarchy of cultural values: Europeans at the very top, Arabs (and probably Asians) somewhere in the middle, Johannese slightly below, and Africans at the very bottom. Even those Africans who had a touch of Arab "blood" are seen as no more than handsome bodies, superior animals devoid of character and intellectual faculties. These, no doubt, have to await cultivation by an external "redeemer," by a civilizing mission from the north, across the seas. It made sense to Prior, therefore, that once the Arabs and Portuguese abandoned their Swahili colonies, the people, left to themselves, would gradually sink "to the barbarism of the original African, existing in small and scattered communities rather than as formerly, in rich and flourishing nations" (Freeman-Grenville, 210).

In stark contrast to the picture of the Swahili presented by Prior, the Swahili depiction of themselves was contained in the Mombasa Chronicle, written at about the same time as Prior's *Voyage in the Nisus Frigate*. In this local history of Mombasa, the Swahili are presented as a clearly identifiable group of people, certainly different from the Arabs, whose strong sense of self-preservation led them to ingeniously play one real or potential colonial power against another. At no point in this chronicle, nor in any of the subsequent local, documented histories of the Swahili people, does the issue of their skin color or their mis-cegenation with Arabs assume any presence at all in the minds of the writers. If there were questions of color and of racial origins they certainly did not seem to be featured in the Swahili consciousness of their identity at that time.

During this period the Swahili were still under a foreign rule that did not establish an administrative seat in Zanzibar until 1832. The Arab rulers were, of course, not unconscious of color. If they seemed naturally liberal in matters of marriage, for example, their liberalism was still racial by virtue of the one-sid-edness of their marital intercourse: "Arab" males with "African" women, seldom the reverse. Arab slavery was not based on color. It was a multiracial slavery.[9] But since it now targeted African peoples exclusively, it naturally assumed a racist dimension. Therefore, it cannot be claimed that the Arab rulers of the Swahili coast had been completely unmindful of color and race in their relationship with the colonized African. After all, the racial subhumanization of the "other," in color and/or cultural terms, becomes an important component of every dominating class, in Africa and elsewhere.

But, as explained earlier, precisely because the Arabs them-selves were so diverse, comprising people of various colors and racial origins, the racial equation in genetic-pigmentational terms could only be stretched so far. Under Arab rule, then, the ideology of the "cultural inferiority" of the "other" was more prominent than the ideology of "racial inferiority." And once cultural assimilation had taken place, once an Arab linguistic and cultural imprint had been "properly" acquired, skin color was automatically subsumed under a vertical paradigm of the Arab "self" in which light skin was favored over dark.

The cultural prejudices of Arab rule naturally had their impact on Swahili conceptions of the "self." It was clear to many Swahili people that the less Arabized they were, in cultural terms, the less they were regarded as complete human beings. The "colonial mentality" of the time among the Swahili, there-fore, was to Arabize culturally and to consider this cultural Arabness a mark of status. If those who were Swahili by virtue of Swahilization from an Arab past came to the forefront of this quest for cultural Arabness, the quest soon became a norm that filtered through to virtually all strata of Swahili society. At the same time, however, this Arabness remained abstract, idealized, and different from that of the "real" Arabs. It was an Arabness that, though partly prompted by Arab rule, found its inspiration in the world of Islam. Moreover, this absolutization of Arab cultural superiority, a specifically nineteenth century phenomenon, certainly intensified a sense of ethnic hierarchy and social stratification. However, so dense have been the many forms of Arab/African intermingling over a great many cultures that there was no analogous line of demarcation between the Arab, the Arabized, and the non-Arab as there had been and continued to be between the European and the non-European.

The Swahili scenario under Arab rule can thus be contrasted with an African scenario under British colonialism. If linguistic and cultural assimilation *per se* could allow a subjugated African to acquire the identity of the Arab master, it was certainly not the case of the African under British colonialism. To be English one had not only to transcend linguistic and cultural assimilation; one also had to be assimilated physically, to acquire the physical attributes of the English. The "colonial mentality" of the African under British colonialism, therefore, expressed itself not only in terms of an attempt to acquire English cultural and linguistic manners, but also, as much as possible, to acquire the physical attributes of the colonial master. Skin lightening by chemical creams such as *Ambi,* and the straightening and coloring of the hair, for example, became some of the manifestations of this colonial hangover, a tendency also observable in the African Diaspora.

Though a lightness of color was in some context more privileged, a darkness of skin color of any Swahili did not militate against acquiring an identity of Arabness once the condition of cultural assimilation had been fulfilled. Under Arab rule the Swahili did not have to subject themselves to this physical self-transformation since skin color was only one element, and often not the *dominant* element, in the Arab modes of constructing hierarchies and social privileges. The issue of lineage was, at least, equally important so that a person of royal lineage, for example, occupied a higher social status than that of common citizenry, regardless of pigmentation; in actual fact, some members of the royal family tended to be darker than average in complexion. There was likewise the issue of cultural assimilation as such which included a whole host of elements, ranging from linguistic mastery to pietistic scholarship and from personal habits to sanctioned public power, which constantly mitigated the efforts of "racial" consciousness. One can say, then, that by the time of the inception of British colonial rule, an *ideal of cultural Arabness* had already emerged in the mind of the Swahili, prompted by Arab rule and probably more so by Islam. This now came to "complement" (or perhaps "confuse") the cultural Arabness that had been organically acquired through the centuries-old Swahili-Arab contact. Since Arab settlers themselves became Swahilized, some Arab elements were bound to infuse Swahili culture.

Swahili identity, then, already confounded by the forces of Arab rule, now came under the influence of British colonial ideology. Prior had already established the foundations of this ideology several decades before British colonial rule in east Africa. With the inception of British colonialism, new colonial ideologues took up the gauntlet. After Prior, A.C. Madan offered a typically Eurocentric definition of Swahili people as "a mixture of African and Arab elements" even though the proportions of the racial mixture are supposed to vary indefinably (1903:v). This was soon followed by Edward Steere's definition of a Swahili as "a man of mixed Negro and Arab descent" (1908:4). Similar definitions, then, were amplified in such scholarly compendia as the *Encyclopaedia Britannica* of 1911. But now the "African blood" running through Swahili veins was no longer seen as an impediment, as Prior once assumed, to the genetic transfer of Arab psycho-cultural traits. On the contrary, these Arab traits are now regarded as part of Swahili identity and, in contrast to other Africans, as constituting Swahili's paramount redeeming factors. According to the *Britannica*:

> The Swahili are essentially a mixed people, the result of long crossing between the Negroes of the coast and the Arabs, with an admixture of slave blood from nearly all the East African tribes. ... The energy and intelligence derived from their Semitic blood have enabled them to take a lead-

ing part in the development of trade and the industries. (1911:117)

The *Encyclopaedia Britannica* thus stakes its reputation on the supposedly dual nature of the Swahili and on the proposition that but for the "Semitic blood" that runs freely in their veins, the Swahili would be expected to be no better than other Africans: ignorant and inert.

An even more alarming proposition about the theory of the dual nature of the Swahili, which came out at about the same time as the *Encyclopaedia Britannica,* is that of Captain Stigand. Probably taking his cue from Edward Steere's observation that "a Swahili by definition is a man of a mixed Negro and Arab descent," Stigand writes:

> The Swahili is cheerful and happy-go-lucky as the African; fond of humour, intrigue and power as the Arab.
>
> Like the Arab, but to an even greater extent, he lives in two separate worlds, one of words and one of deeds.
>
> If you judge him by his sentiments, you find a man of noble aspirations, lofty ideals, intelligent thoughts, devout, kind, sympathetic and honourable.
>
> If you judge him by his actions, however, you find a man low, sordid, cunning, thieving, slanderous, callous and ignorant. For instance, he will say, "A man's mother is his second God," and then will disown his mother entirely because she is not of the same class as his father, and perhaps beat her if she comes near him.
>
> For the proper understanding of the savage African, one must not look on him as a human being, but as a rather superior kind of animal. Looked on from this point of view, many of his actions and ways of thought are intelligible, where otherwise they are inexplicable. To judge the African side of the Swahili nature he must be looked at from this standpoint. However, he has another side, the Arab side, a much more complex quality to understand. (Stigand, 1913:130)

The reader's first response to Stigand's remarks would probably be to dismiss him as a racist. Yet Captain Stigand was not simply a "bad bigot." His was a racist age, and he can at best be faulted for recording for posterity, in most incisive language, what Europeans were saying and thinking about other peoples, especially those inhabitants of the "dark continent," in the early decades of this eventful century. Moreover, Stigand served in east Africa as the imperial servant of Great Britain, the most dominant power of a dominant Europe, whose empire had just been constructed on the back of a large section of humankind. And it follows that a dominant people like the British of the early twentieth century were intoxicated, precisely by reason of their dominance, by notions of racial superiority and uniqueness.

According to Stigand, the Swahili is a perpetual schizophrenic, forever divided between his two quite disparate souls, one African and the other Arab. In addition, if Prior found the Swahili personality to be lacking in any of the positive Arab characteristics, due to the resilience of the African side of Swahili blood, and if the Encyclopaedia Britannica found it endowed with honorable Arab attributes due to the people's history of miscegenation with Arabs, Stigand found the two bloodstreams to have a mutually neutralizing effect on each other. In Stigand's order of racial hierarchy the African was only "a superior kind of animal," while the Arab was, at best, an inferior kind of human. With this equation — the African as the best of animals, the Arab as the worst of human beings — the Swahili represent both and neither. Whatever the case, the trend that stressed the "Arab nature" of Swahili identity had now been set in motion by Germanic racist conceptions of "self" and "other." It became a trend that caught on like wildfire and, as we shall illustrate, fitted well with the colonial designs of the British.

When the British invaded east Africa, they were in an era of expanding industrial capitalism that needed colonial expansion. The industrial revolution, which began in Britain, quickly rendered slave labor obsolete. Slavery, therefore, had to be abolished partly to pave the way for the development and consolidation of capitalism on the global scale. This is not to suggest, of course, that the entire British "abolitionist movement" was based on politico-economic considerations; there were indeed abolitionists' efforts that were motivated primarily by humanitarian concerns. But the politico-economic equation was certainly the more basic underlying factor in the British government's global strategy to see slavery abolished.

But capitalism cannot go about declaring its *reality* to the world, even in efforts that seem philanthropic: to plunder and loot on a global scale, to bring some to the center and push others to the periphery of capitalist production. To do so would delegitimize capitalism and undermine the very foundations upon which it is erected as a world system. Capitalism rather, like any other economic system, creates an ideology, a set of myths so to speak, from which it draws its legitimacy, and with which it can cover its inherent inequity. Without such an ideology, capitalism would allow the exposure of its own internal contradictions and thereby create doubt about its eternity, its consonance with the "nature" of man. A dominant capitalist ideology, therefore, "must remove this type of destructive doubt from its field of vision. It must succeed in affirming itself as a system founded on 'eternal truths' with transhistorical vocation" (Amin, 76).

One of the myths of capitalist ideology that is of direct relevance hinges on the abstraction of the achievements of capitalist development from their historical context. What are in fact universal tendencies of human evolution, given a certain conjunction of historical forces, are now presented as a uniquely European phenomenon. Europeans are now given a mythical historical unity beyond time and space, a mythical history that pits a "civilized" self against an "uncivilized" other. The "white man's burden" with its civilizing mission to Africa and other "uncivilized" parts of the world has its origins in this calculated historical distortion that became a part of capitalist ideology.

In east Africa, specifically, imperial capitalism also found it expedient to capitalize on the history of Arab slavery in the construction of its legitimating ideology. If European and American slavery was grossly underplayed and virtually excused in British education of the "native," Arab slavery was grossly exaggerated in its form, magnitude, and cruelty. By so doing, the British could now draw on their history of the movement to abolish slavery, to march into the eastern region of Africa, not only as a people with a great civilizing mission by virtue of their Europeanness, but also as Africa's redeemers from Arab bondage.[10] The urge to depict the Arab as an irredeemable villain, then, became irresistible, compelling, to the imperial capitalist ideology of the time.

Imperial capitalist ideology that emphasized a unity of Europeans was not restricted, however, to the area of race. It also extended to the sphere of religion. This became particularly important in the twentieth century when nationalist sentiments were putting heavy stress on European differences. Christianity as the dominant religion in Europe was suddenly discovered as the eternal tie that would continue to bind the Europeans. Another historical myth was thus created that attempted to link religion with race. Christianity thus became European; Islam was bound to Arab identity; "Animism" became uniquely African; Asians were accorded their own unique religions, and so forth. This was projected as the reality despite the fact that Christianity was "Oriental" and African long before it set foot on any European soil. Furthermore, Christianity itself had to be assimilated into a Eurocentric teleology. As Samir Amin points out:

> The Holy Family and the Egyptian and Syrian Church Fathers had to be made European. Non-Christian Ancient Greece also had to be assimilated into this lineage. . . . But above all, the uniqueness of Christianity had to be magnified and adorned with particular and exclusive virtues that, by simple teleology, account for the superiority of the West and its conquest of other peoples. (99)

The British then arrived in east Africa with this religious conception of their race that quickly became the initial cornerstone of their "civilizing" mission and colonial ideology. To their dismay they discovered that Islam had already "captured" the souls of many Africans and had the potential of continuing to do so in direct conflict with the interests of the Christian missionary enterprise. The British became more concerned about this situation because elsewhere (as in the case of Somalia, Morocco, Libya, and the Yao of Malawi) Islam had served as an important ideological force of resistance against European colonialism. The efforts to equate Islam with Arabness were thus intensified and subsequently the evil slave system of the Arabs was extended to "their" religion. Henceforth, the Swahili became a target of a two-pronged attack: one against their Arab connection and the other against their Islamic connection. Fires of disaffection and disunity were, therefore, fanned around abstracted Arab and Islamic components of Swahili identity, fires that threatened the very survival of the Swahili organism. Against the background of Arab rule, and Arab-Islamic cultural superordination, British imperialism regarded Arabs and Muslims as one of the major contradictions in their east African imperial designs, at least in the early stages of British colonialism. The subhumanization of people with Arab and Islamic connections, therefore, became a component of the ideological arsenal of British colonialism. And it is against this backdrop that we must understand the sentiments expressed by people like Stigand.

If the colonial efforts to overplay the element of Arabness in Swahili identity ultimately affected inter- and intra-Swahili relations, colonial efforts to exaggerate the Islamicness of Swahili identity affected mainly outer-group relations with the Swahili. Because of the predominantly Islamic composition of the Swahili community, the view developed that to be a Swahili was to be a Muslim. From this a counter-irrationality developed, that, for an east African to be a Muslim was to be a Swahili. A trend was thus set whereby many east Africans who adopted the Islamic religion took upon themselves the Swahili ethnic label. Christianized Africans became merely "imitation Europeans." But the colonial politics fostered a situation in which Muslim Africans supposedly became not imitation but real Swahili at the primary stage — virtually losing their original ethnic identity — and more indirectly, Arab.

But how necessary, in fact, is Islam as a condition for Swahili identity? There has definitely been quite a bit of controversy over this issue even among the Swahili people themselves. Ali A. Mazrui, for example, considers Islam as an accompanying characteristic of Swahili identity (1989: 95). A. S. Nabhany and M. Kamal Khan, on the other hand, contend that it is not at all necessary to be a Muslim to be a member of the Swahili nationality (1978). Our own position, however, is that it is not Islam as a *religion* that counts in Swahili identity. It is rather Islam as a grid of cultural practices. There are individuals, though still numerically insignificant, who are ethnically Swahili but non-Muslim in religious affiliation. But invariably such people maintain Swahili-Islamic cultural practices in virtually all spheres of life except that of worship. A general Islamic cultural horizon, therefore, and not Islam as a faith, seems to be one of the binding factors in Swahili identity. This also accounts for the brand of Arabness that seems to be featured in Swahili identity — an Arabness coinciding with certain aspects of Islam, not inherent in the Arab people as such. Despite these qualifications, however, this Islamicness and Arabness of the Swahili continued to be featured in the colonial ideology that sought to associate Islam with slavery and Euro-Christianity with freedom.

But, of course, any legitimating ideology would not survive if it is not imbibed by the objects and victims of that system. If British imperial ideology was to gain credibility among Africans, for example, it could not be seen to be espoused and articulated only by the likes of Prior, Stigand, and Steere. It also needed recruits from within the ranks of Africans themselves. This is perhaps where the story of James Juma Mbotela becomes revelant.

James Juma Mbotela was born of parents who were among the people supposedly freed by the British and settled in Frere Town in Kisauni, Mombasa, on the coast of Kenya. In the process they became Christians. James Mbotela himself grew up with Swahili as his first language. He eventually joined the Christian Church as an evangelist. Reminiscing about the experiences of his parents, James Mbotela produced in 1934 a book written in Swahili entitled *Uhuru wa Watumwa* (*Freedom of the Slaves*), which was quickly adopted as a reader in schools. The singular objective of this text was to give concrete substance, from the African experience, to the colonial portrayal of the Swahili, the Arabs, and the Muslims as villains and peddlers of slaves, while portraying the British as God-sent saviors.

But a close examination of the book raises significant doubts about its authorship. For example, the Swahili language was native to Mbotela. Yet the book is written in a language that is not at all easy to read for a native speaker of Swahili. The Swahili, therein, lacks a natural flow or spontaneity and is virtually bare of Swahili idioms and diction that carry important nuances. Quite often the sentences become fully intelligible after they are translated into English. In short it becomes difficult to believe that this book was written by a person with a native proficiency in the Swahili language. It seems probable that the book is either a bad translation from an English original, or that it was written in Swahili by a person other than Mbotela, by a person who does not have Mbotela's command of the Swahili language. It may well be that, consonant with his Christian evangelical zeal, Mbotela allowed the book to be issued in his name so as to give the British ideological campaign against the Arabs, against the Swahili, and the Muslims in general, an African stamp. This may explain why the book was reprinted several times and turned into a primary Swahili reader in many east African schools. The objective was to influence an entire generation of African leaders in their attitudes towards Islam, the Swahili, and Arabs.

But if the Swahili were discredited essentially because of their Arab-Islamic heritage, other Africans suffered British abuse by virtue of their Africanness. Thus Africanity became synonymous with extreme racial inferiority, with primitiveness and barbarism. Thus the impression was created that no people were more deserving of British racial segregation and more in need of the British civilizing mission than those of African origin. This divisive, racist ideology of European superiority in a hierarchy of racial orders was then canonized into British imperial law quite early in the British colonial experience in east Africa. As A. I. Salim commented:

> Discriminating laws were introduced into the East Africa Protectorate from an early date. One yardstick with which one can measure a discriminating ordinance was by the use of the term "native" or "non-native." Thus as years passed, the more one was native to the country, the more underprivileged one was. Thus when it came to introducing taxation in 1901, it was the indigenous who were taxed first. These were described as "natives" in the Native Hut Tax Ordinance of that year. Arabs and Waswahili were to all intents and purposes regarded then as a homogenous body, all natives, like the African, paying the Hut Tax of Rupees. (3)

"Native," then, not only came to mean primitive and inferior, but also a category of economic liability tied to colonial taxation.

At that stage the British colonial administration found no contradiction in regarding the Arabs of the Kenya coast as "native" to the region. Since the British were at that time still engaged in their ideological onslaught against Arab and Muslims in east Africa, the inclusion of "Arabs" in the native category would justify the same level and kind of discrimination as was meted out to other "natives." At that point, therefore, Stigand's conception of African and Arab identity in terms of a thin line between "the highest of animals" and "the lowest of humans" still reigned supreme in the British imperial ideology, and serious distinction between the two was deemed unwarranted for any practical purposes. However, once the British felt firmly positioned on their east African imperial saddle and had ceased to regard the Muslim coastalists as an impending source of militant opposition to British rule, realizing, instead, that east African Islam was not such a missionary religion, after all, as to pose a threat to the spread of Christianity among other "natives," the subhumanization of the Arab could now be moderated. Better still Arabness could now be given an ideological thrust that would be in accord with the growing British strategy of divide and rule.

In the meantime, "nativeness," as defined in British colonial law, had started playing havoc on the coast of Kenya. If "nativeness" meant "taxation," if it meant "inferior" food in smaller quantities in periods of food rationing, if it generally meant fewer and less favorable privileges within the colonial system, then "nativeness" had certainly become a plague from which one could escape only by obtaining the status of "non-native" in colonial law. These considerations prompted a struggle among sections of Arab settlers for "non-native" status, which held out the promise of power and privilege over the "native" population. Under these circumstances, many Swahili soon found themselves clamoring for "non-native" status, for non-local origins, some claiming Arab ancestry, others Asian ancestry of one sort or another.

It is a conjunction of these two tendencies — the waning British fears of an Islamic militant resistance against their rule, and mounting Swahili fears about the consequences of their "nativeness" — that ultimately led to a reconceptualization of the colonial categories of "native" and "non-native." According to Salim:

> "Native" was now interpreted to be any person "one of [whose] parents is a member of an indigenous African tribe or community, in which term are included people known as the Waswahili, but the term native shall not include (a) an Arab, an Abyssinian, a Somali, a Baluchi born in Africa, a Malagasy or a Comoro Islander"; or (b) any person who "of his own motion proved to the satisfaction of the magistrate of the subordinate court that he was of 'non-native' descent." (4)

This law is rather interesting for a couple of important reasons. It begins by accepting a premise that is quite in conformity with both African and Arab paradigms of identity, but not that of Europeans, that either paternal or maternal African parentage would automatically qualify a person for a "native" identity. Then it proceeds to exclude from this same definition of "native," not only Arabs but also certain categories of Africans, namely Abyssinians, Somalis, and the Ngazija (Comorians), even when *both* parents are in fact African. A Kenyan Somali whose parents are Kenyan Somali would thus be "non-native" to Kenya and exempt from "native" laws, but a Pokomo whose father is a Zulu from South Africa would still be considered a "native" and subject to native law.

But what is that common factor that binds Arabs, Somalis, Abyssinians, Baluchis, Malagasies, and Comorians, while distinguishing them from "natives"? Their "non-Negro" origins, according to the divisive classifications of European anthropologists and linguists. The Arabs and some Abyssinians were "Semitic," the Somalis and some Abyssinians were said to be "Hamitic,"[11] the Baluchis and Malagasies were Asiatic, and so forth. So even people who were distinctly African in every imaginable sense of the word, were now divided, in order of superiority, into "Semitic," "Hamitic," and "Negroid" stocks. The native was now the lowest of the low, a member of the lowest "sub-race" of the lowest "race" in the Eurocentric hierarchy. And it is in this category that the Swahili were included.

The British, however, having been forced to discard some of

their prejudices against Arabs and Islam by the changing political dynamics of the region, now came to adopt a conception of the Swahili somewhat akin to the one encapsulated in the *Encyclopaedia Britannica*. The long history of contact with the somewhat "superior race" of Arabs and with the monotheism of Islam was now regarded as an asset rather than a liability in Swahili history. The Swahili, therefore, unlike other "Negroes" were provided with a legal loophole through which some of them could escape the scourge of their nativeness, if they so desired. This loophole is the legal provision that people who, of their own volition, would satisfy a magistrate of a subordinate colonial court that they had "non-native" blood, would cease to be categorized as "native."

This law had two important effects insofar as the history of Swahili identity is concerned. First, in view of the system of taxation and the disproportionate allocation of materials, services, and privileges along "native"/"non-native" lines, the law encouraged the Swahili to reject their indigenous origins. Some Swahili assumed new family names, others claimed Arab ancestry where they had none, while some others combined the two strategies, all in a desperate attempt to satisfy magistrates of subordinate courts that, in fact, they had "non-native" origins and should be accorded "non-native" status.

Second, the law planted dangerous seeds of disunity among the Swahili. If they had in the past always considered themselves as one people, with a sense of common destiny despite their variation in origins and color, this was now shattered at the altar of British colonial expediency. The Swahili community was divided into mythical Arab, Afro-Arab, and African components that could no longer be in harmony with one another. And the competition for meager and disproportionately allocated resources naturally led to intra-Swahili tensions and conflicts, sometimes bordering on bloodshed, that almost split the Swahili organism asunder. This problem was further aggravated by British use of "Arab" intermediaries in the colonial administration of their coastal dominions.

Further confusion was created by inconsistencies in colonial law. If, as indicated above, the new civil law regarded Arabs as "non-native" and therefore privileged, under the Criminal Procedure Ordinance of 1914, which existed alongside that civil law, the same Arabs were treated as "native" and therefore less privileged. This ordinance defined a "native" as any local person of non-European or non-Asian origin. Thus a combination of colonial laws introduced an element of duality, a pervasive ambiguity, in the legal identity of both Africans and Arabs albeit on different planes. And this confusion was naturally compounded in the case of the Swahili owing precisely to their "dual heritage." If Africans were both "native" (Negroid) and "non-native" ("Semites" and "Hamites"), what happens to the Swahili collectivity that included within its rank people of "Negroid," "Semitic," and "Hamitic" descent? And if the Arabs are both "non-native" (under civil law) and "native" (under criminal law), what is the status of the Swahili who have renounced their nativeness by assuming an Arab identity? Colonial law had thus precipitated an identity crisis of tremendous magnitude among the Swahili. And if Swahili identity has survived to this day, which it has, it only attests to the resilience of Swahili consciousness among the people themselves.

This already beleaguered Swahili identity was thrown, then, into an even deeper vortex of confusion by the vagaries of the colonial political economy. If the tax ordinance of 1900 lumped Arabs and Swahili together and classified them as natives, and if the 1910 amendment of the same ordinance treated Arabs and Swahili as separate people, colonial regulations of the years that followed turned into a tossing game that drove a further wedge among the Swahili. In particular, the colonial position kept shifting as regards the identity of a section of the Swahili, the *Ithnashara Taifa* (Twelve Tribes), the indigenes of Mombasa island, who would get periodically tossed into an African-native category, then into an Arab-non-native category, then back into an African category, and so forth. Meanwhile, some other sections of the Swahili — the *Thalatha Taifa* (Three Tribes of Mombasa mainland), the Bajuni, and others — continued to be treated as African and therefore native. The disorder that was thus created by the ambiguities of colonial law regarding Arab identity on the one hand, and African identity on the other, was applied with special force to the Swahili in connection with the natives of Mombasa island, and its multifaceted trappings persisted throughout the colonial period and even flowed in a torrent into the neocolonial dispensation.

The colonial legacy in connection with Swahili identity had far-reaching consequences in at least five different ways. There is first the response of European scholars like A.H. Prins, Lyndon Harries, and Jan Knappert, who, perhaps unconsciously, served as the Eurocentric mediating ideologues between the colonial and neocolonial phases. In connection with Swahili identity, therefore, they continued to harp on the two-nature theory, though in divergent ways. Knappert, for example, wrote authoritatively, yet unquestioningly:

> . . . it seems justifiable to picture Swahili society of those days as essentially similar to what it is today. Recent immigrants of Arabia and India mingled with recent immigrants from the Bantu interior gradually to blend into that uniquely new race: the Swahili, neither African nor Asian, but *sui gereris*, an open society, tolerant and free. (1979: 110)

Knappert, unlike Stigand and more like the the *Encyclopaedia Britannica*, does not begrudge the Swahili their humanity, their positive qualities — open, tolerant, and free — which he attributes nevertheless to a putative Arab factor in their blood. Knappert's has been a distinguished career of research and writing on Swahili life and lore, and he is deservedly famous for assembling and disseminating a very considerable archive of Swahili poetry. It would therefore be unfair to accuse him of anti-Swahili sentiments. Yet by denying the Swahili their Africanity, by treating them as a "race" different and separate from other African groups, he not only sowed potential seeds of disunity, but also placed powerful intellectual ammunition in the hands of those inclined to disenfranchise the Swahili people. Furthermore, Knappert has compounded the confusions regarding Swahili identity even further by linking it to the evasive category of "race."

It is not only the racism of the colonial tradition, however, that we witness in some of the writings of this first group of scholars. There is also a strand reminiscent of colonial politics connected with the history of slavery. In the introduction to his three-volume study of Swahili Islamic poetry, for example, Knappert writes:

> From the economic point of view the Islamic civilization of the East African coast was based entirely on the slavery system. Slaves built the houses and palaces, slaves worked the plantations, slaves carried the gold and ivory from the interior; and these two commodities, as well as copper, account for the very existence of Islamic culture on the coast. (1971: 4)

One of the authors of this current text (Shariff, 1971 and 1984) has already demonstrated how Knappert developed a characteristic tendency of using adjectives of extremity, sometimes "positive," sometimes "negative," in his depiction of the Swahili and their culture. The idea that the Swahili Islamic civilization was based entirely on slave labor, therefore, must be seen with this Knappertian syndrome in mind. In addition, however, Knappert's position is in contradiction with historical findings. No Swahili slaves or non-slaves are known to have ventured into the interior prior to the nineteenth century. As Chittick observes, "goods were brought to the coast by the people of the interior; there is hardly any evidence of expeditions inland until the nineteenth century" (1969: 108-109). Until that point, therefore, if there was any slave labor on the Swahili coast, it was certainly not central to the flourishing trade in ivory and other commodities from the hinterland. And it was not until the nineteenth century that slave labor came to be used at all on the Swahili coast for local production. It was the final abolition of the slave trade internationally that led to the exploitation of slave labor locally. Abdul Sheriff, who has done extensive research on the subject, explains that the "loss of the market for slaves in French sugar colonies, in the Mescarenes and in the Americas, had encouraged Arab slave traders to divert that labour to the clove plantations of Zanzibar when clove prices were extremely attractive, and later to the grain plantations on the East African coast" (1987: 275). And, according to Nicholls, this use of slave labor in local production and trade was not a phenomenon of the entire Swahili society; it was, rather, restricted to sections of the Arab and Swahili "bourgeoisie." (25)

Yet a pervasive Islamic culture had already been firmly established on the Swahili coast well before the nineteenth century.

If slave labor did not become significant in the east African coastal economy until well into the nineteenth century, then, it is difficult to understand how it could have led, in Knappert's words, to "the very existence of Islamic culture on the coast." Some controllers of the means of production, of agricultural plantation among Arab settlers, among the Swahili, the Giriama, the Baganda, and some other African peoples, were prompted by the economics of their time to use slave labor for local production. Yet the nature of that slavery, and the relatively short duration in which it came to feature in economic production, can hardly be considered to account for the very emergence of the respective cultures of these people.

What Knappert tried to do here is to transpose what has been said of American society — that it was erected on the backs of African slaves — to the Swahili coast. In essence, this is a neo-colonial ideological ploy intended to defuse the whole issue of African slave exploitation, which had been peculiar to the Americas, by giving to that kind of slavery a semblance of universality. By pointing to an African civilization supposedly built on slave labor, neocolonial ideologues like Knappert hoped to demonstrate, at least to their own satisfaction, that the white American conduct had been analogous to, and no worse than, that of the Arab/Islamic/Swahili on the east Africa coast.

The second response to the colonially created confusion about Swahili identity was that of the more modern research-oriented scholar interested in a "scientific" answer to the question, Who are the Swahili? The "confusion" over Swahili identity came to serve as a lucrative research area for aspiring "Africanists." Most exemplary in this Eurocentric trend of scholarship is probably the article, quoted earlier, by Carol Eastman (1971). The cumulative effect of much of this kind of scholarship, however, has again been to add to (rather than reduce) the confusion about Swahili identity. The colonial categories pertaining to Swahili identity were now multiplied and capped with binary features by modern and peculiarly Eurocentric empiricism. The end result, of course, was to raise further doubt about the substance and indeed the very reality of Swahili identity.

The chaos created by colonialism, and the doubts raised by modern scholars, naturally led then to a "Kenya government position," which may be regarded as the third response to the question of Swahili identity. Mainly for political-economic reasons, which we shall have the opportunity to discuss in the conclusion, sections of the Kenya administration adopted a position that essentially rejected the existence of Swahili as a definable, cohesive community of people. While this position has remained unarticulated for the most part and is seen mainly in practice when members of the Swahili community attempt to apply for passports or identity cards, one gets a glimpse of it in the publications of the Kenya Ministry of Tourism and Wildlife. In one leaflet, the Ministry asserts:

> There is no such thing as Swahili tribe or group; the term is loosely applied to a variety of people who live on Kenya's coast who are linked only by their common language and to an extent, a common religion — Islam. (TSM\SM-23)

In the minds of many Kenyan government officials, in fact, those who had all along regarded themselves as Swahili were merely local "Arabs." If the colonial government of Kenya, in one of its trajectories, lumped the Swahili with the Arabs and considered them native to the land about ninety years ago, some members of the neocolonial government of Kenya now lumped the Swahili with the Arab and considered them all "non-native," alien to the region. This Kenyan government position about Swahili identity now passed and caught on as the "eternal truth." As we shall show later, the ideological foundations of Swahili disenfranchisement in the neocolonial era had now been properly set.

The Kenyan government has not been completely consistent in its position about the Swahili, however. For example, the Central Bureau of Statistics has included Swahili as an ethnic category in its census reports since 1979. But this demographic activity can hardly claim any influence on governmental policy towards the Swahili, or much popular support among non-Swahili Kenyans, so that it remains a mere statistical digit, while in the dominant discourse of the Kenyan state "Swahili" has remained a label without a definable people.

If in capitalist Kenya the Swahili were denied an identity by the extinction of the very notion of "Swahili identity," the socialist policies of Tanzania resulted in the opposite tendency, the tendency to generalize Swahili identity beyond the frontiers of Swahili ethnicity. At least in what is sometimes called Tanganyika (mainland Tanzania), therefore, the term Swahili has often come to refer to virtually any person of African origin in that general region. We have been told that it became a matter of policy in Tanzania to discourage any writings that claim an independent Swahili ethnicity distinct from other ethnicities within the country. Swahiliness was thus arbitrarily expanded in the quest for a wider national identity. But in both Kenya and Tanzania, despite their differences in strategy, the end result was the same: the Swahili people as an ethnic group ceased to be recognized as such, and the ideological foundations for their disenfranchisement had been set. Whatever the case, the Tanzanian position constitutes the fourth kind of response to the colonial legacy around the question of Swahili identity: In Kenya, Swahili ethnicity is non-existent, because no one is considered Swahili; in Tanzania, because everyone is considered Swahili.

There is, of course, another fundamental political difference between Tanzanian and Kenyan "policies" on the question of Swahili identity. Tanzanian policy is seemingly based on "progressive" concerns that affect not only the Swahili but virtually all other ethnic groups in the country. The Swahili are "required" to give up their ethnic identity so that it can be turned into the public property of the Tanzanian nation. The non-Swahili members of Tanzania, on the other hand, are required to relinquish their own ethnic identities in order to imbibe a wider and collective identity under a Swahili label. This two-pronged unarticulated policy, however, has been pursued on the terms of the Tanzanian state and not of the Tanzanian people; it has been pursued bureaucratically and not democratically. Regardless of the bureaucratic nature of the initiative to redefine the boundaries of Swahili identity, however, there is little doubt that a new Swahili identity is in the making, at least in mainland Tanzania. This process has been catalyzed by three main factors. First, the rigorous promotion of Swahili has led to an increasing proportion of Tanzanians growing up speaking the language as their first tongue. Second, an Islamic ethos, which is usually associated with Swahili identity, has been internalized by many Tanzanians. Third, the quasi-socialist policies of the country have tended to neutralize the possibility of mass exclusion of any particular ethnic community from politico-economic participation. The combination of these factors, then, may have expedited the "Swahilization" of the Tanzanian population to a point where the demographic ranks of the Swahili can be said to be on the increase.

Despite these seeming differences between Tanzania and Kenya, however, their policies may in fact have been derived from a common misconception. In particular, the Tanzanian policy may also have been informed by the prevailing Kenyan attitude towards Swahili identity; i.e., that there is no Swahili "tribe." It is possible that Swahili identity was deemed "nationalizable" in Tanzania, not only because the Swahili language had spread extensively in that country, but also because Swahili was seen as a label without a discernible people. Beginning with the same presupposition about Swahili identity, then, the quasisocialist ideology of Tanzania favored its greater centralization, while the quasicapitalist ideology of Kenya sought its greater marginalization. But precisely because both these ideologies are rooted in neocolonial political economies, their end result, as the Swahili on both sides of the border seem to believe, has been the same.

The fifth kind of response took the form of a reaction against the positions discussed so far. It is a reaction with a "Swahili nationalist" thrust that insists that the Swahili do exist not only as a people, but also that their identity is primarily African. The most prominent proponents of this position have, of course, come from within the ranks of the Swahili people themselves. In his critique (1971) of Knappert's work on traditional Swahili poetry, one of the authors of this text, for example, challenges the one-sided, Arab-oriented claims about Swahili identity. And in his recent book, he (Shariff, 1988) exposes the racism inherent in Eurocentric categorizations of African peoples in general, and of the Swahili in particular.

Some of the Swahili "nationalists" have tended to play down the element of Swahili ethnicity and emphasize instead the cultural unity of the people. But in responding to a popular sentiment, such as that of Kenya's Ministry of Tourism and Wildlife, that Swahili is not a "tribe," Chiraghdin (1974:6) puts forward a passionate argument that the Swahili do in fact constitute a "tribe" in any of the following senses of the word: (1) a group of people who claim a specific ancestry, i.e., having their own clans and lineages; (2) a nation of people, united, who have the same traditions that distinguish them from others, i.e., having their own customs, their own beliefs, their own culture, their own mores that determine their mode of interaction in weddings, funerals, circumcision ceremonies, and so forth; (3) a group of people who have the same language and literature that reflect their thoughts and creative genius, in oral and written form; (4) a group of people who live in the same geographical area, i.e., having more or less the same environmental conditions to which they have adjusted their lives.

To Chiraghdin and most other Swahili nationalists, then, the Swahili not only exist, but are an African people in terms of their geographical origins, in terms of the criteria and categories that are applicable in defining other African collectivities, and in relation to their cultural forms and institutions, which they have evolved for themselves and which are in every way comparable to those of other groups on the continent.

One argument that is often raised to justify the claim that the Swahili are a non-native unit is their "ethnically mixed" character. But if an offspring of Maasai-Indian parentage can be considered ethnically Maasai, or that of European-Kalenjin as ethnically Kalenjin, why should the offspring of Swahili-Arab, Swahili-Asian, or Swahili-Giriama intermarriages be considered any less ethnically Swahili? Cross-ethnic intermarriages are, in fact, legion in Africa and the language and culture to which the offspring is exposed usually determines its ethnic identity. Why should this resilience of the African paradigm of identity suddenly cease in the case of the Swahili? Clearly, there is a political dynamic at work here, to which we shall return later.

The Swahili nationalists have not been alone in their ideological struggle. They have had the support of some other African people, and also of some European (including American) scholars who are attempting to undo the damage done by their predecessors. In this group we may include people like W. Arens (1975), J. de V. Allen (1981), and Derek Nurse and Thomas Spear (1985). Nurse and Spear probably go furthest in their claims. Employing a historical linguistic methodology, they argue that "the Swahili are an African people, born of that continent and raised in it" (1985:viii). But in the same breath they contradict themselves when, after discussing the Swahili participation in the great current of world civilization since the medieval period, they conclude that, "the result has been neither African nor Arab but distinctly Swahili" (1985:viii). Thus, the Swahili are, yet again, denied their Africanity. So even the most liberal Northern scholars seem to be unable to break away from the shackles of the Eurocentric conception of people in terms of "purities," "impurities," and "mixtures." The terminology of the lifeless science of chemistry keeps on being misapplied to the living crucible of humankind!

Some of these nationalists hold views that, in fact, betray their sentiments of racial purism. They make futile attempts to draw a distinction between "pure" and "impure" Swahili. "Pure" Swahili are supposedly those whose ancestry is wholly indigenous to the Swahili coast, while the "impure" ones are said to have a certain amount of "foreign blood." The racism that has informed European ethnographic scholarship on the Swahili in particular, and on human society at large, has thus come to win some adherents within the Swahili community itself.

The Swahili nationalist position and that of its supporters probably constitutes the highest point so far in the ideological counteroffensive around the question of Swahili identity. This was to be expected; it is in a sense a natural intellectual development in the wake of "African nationalism" in the aftermath of colonial racism and divisiveness. The essentially Eurocentric "thesis" that made a fetish of the Swahili's Arabness naturally bore an "antithesis" that makes a fetish of the Swahili's Africanness. The result has been a position that is strongly affirmative about the Swahili's Africanity but virtually apologetic about their Arab links.

What emerges from all this, then, is that the Eurocentric and especially the Germanic paradigm of identity that came to Africa with European colonialism has, in fact, prevailed. Virtually all the views discussed so far, dating from the inception of European colonial rule, have been drawn into the "racial" prison-house that sees Swahili identity in terms of an Arab-African opposition, in terms of a polarity between an alien "racial" origin and a local "racial" origin. Thus Eurocentricism has not only set the terms of the debate on Swahili identity but has also, in the process, consumed our intellectual autonomy to counterpoise it with an Afrocentric methodology. This capitulation to a Eurocentric paradigm of identity, so to speak, is, of course, part and parcel of that wider syndrome of intellectual dependency precipitated by the colonial and neocolonial experiences in Africa, rooted in the interests of global capitalism.

Intellectual dependency manifests itself both in "action" and "reaction." The colonial and neocolonial states, churches, and schools have long been in concert in attempting to raise up to a hegemonic status the capitalist ideology that endows Europeans with an innate and a unique pioneering role in moving the frontiers of world civilization. This ideological hegemony, then, exacts from its victims unsolicited admission of the centrality of Europeans in human civilization. By implication, therefore, European paradigms that have evolved under very specific historical conditions and contexts are projected as universal human paradigms and are accepted as such. To a large extent, intellectual activity in Africa, to this day, betrays this racist ideological hegemony that acknowledges the (European) particular as the (human) universal. And the now familiar quest for Afrocentric paradigms in socio-political thought, in economic thought, in literature, in culture, and so forth is all a response to this state of intellectual dependency.

But a perspective is Eurocentric not only when it shows a pro-European bias. It can also be Eurocentric even when it shows an anti-European or counter-European bias if, in fact, it accepts the Eurocentric terms of debate. It is in this sense that we can regard some African intellectual reactions to the European ideological hegemony as essentially Eurocentic.

A good example of this Eurocentric intellectual reaction to Eurocentricism is the intellectual debate revolving around Africa's contributions to, and African origins of, world civilization. One of the components of Eurocentric ideology has been the myth of uninterrupted Greek ancestry of Europeans, an ancestry that is supposedly the fountain of Western civilization. Thus, the beginnings of scientific and rational thinking became Greek and ultimately, beginning with the Renaissance, uniquely European. Even the period of Islamic enlightenment is presented as having been no more than a transmission belt of ideas from a Greek past to a Renaissance Europe. Ancient Greek literature, however, showed clear connections between Greece and Africa, specifically Egypt. This was a contradiction that was resolved by rejecting the existence of any Greek-African connections and encapsulating Western civilization exclusively in Greco-Roman cultural and "racial" terms. But, just in case, the ideologues of Eurocentricity proceeded to Europeanize Egyptians, to paint the Egyptian aristocracy white and Caucasian.

More recently, however, this European claim of Greek ancestry has come under heavy criticism. Martin Bernal (1987), for example, has exposed the mythical nature of this claim by tracing the history of what he calls the "fabrication of Ancient Greece." He shows that, in fact, ancient Greeks considered themselves as belonging to the same cultural area as the Egyptians and Phoenicians, and that they even claimed Egyptian ancestry. It is said that as much as fifty percent of the Greek tongue had Egyptian and Phoenician linguistic sources. But, in an attempt to deny these Egyptian origins of the Greeks, linguists invented a mysterious "proto-Aryan" language to take the place of this borrowing, thereby safeguarding a myth so dear to Eurocentricism, that of the "Aryan purity of Greece" (Amin, 93).

Having shattered the myth of "Aryan" origins of Western civilization, and having established the Egyptian and, therefore, African foundations of that same civilization, the debate now shifted to the question of the "racial" constitution of those early Egyptians. Yet the conception of people in terms of race and color is essentially European, and to try to prove, as Cheikh Anta Diop (1974) does, that ancient Africans of Egypt were "Negroes" or "black" is to operate within the confines of Eurocentricity. It is to accept the European terms of the debate that "race" and color are, in fact, central in the construction of human civilization. What Martin Bernal calls the "Afro-asiatic" heritage has, in fact, never been bound by European-derived concepts of color and "race" which emerged in post-Renaissance Europe, and to accept these notions in assessing Africa's contribution to world civilization is, in our opinion, to play right into the hands of Eurocentricism.

Like the Africans of Egypt, in a sense the Swahili were participants in a transcontinental historical encounter of great magnitude. In the process they helped to give rise to an architecture, a poetry, a music, a style, indeed a whole new dimension to east African civilization. At the same time participation in this trade contributed to the flowering of the Middle Ages. The Swahili, in a sense, "helped to lay the groundwork for the 10th century renaissance in Europe" (Horton, 1987:86). The Swahili thus served as a link in a chain of African peoples that did, and continue to, contribute to world civilization. Additionally, they assimilated into their ranks, irrespective of color or creed, people of diverse origins and backgrounds. They were thus able to expand their own horizons without assuming the identities of those with whom they interacted, for to have done so would have caused a serious dislocation of the Swahili organism with all its pains and tribulations. The Swahili expanded the horizons of their human experience without compromising their Africanity, since to have done so would have destroyed the very fabric of their collective identity.

What emerged in cultural form cannot be classified in terms of the African-Arab opposition qualifiable only by conjunctions like "either/or," "both," or "neither." It was rather mother Africa's organic birth event, an African encounter with the world around it, a continent flexing itself outward in a concatenation of powerful throbbings — silently, rhythmically, and in perfect harmony. It was the African organism evolving new extensions and continuities in historical time and space. The much publicized Arabness of the Swahili, as indicated earlier, is an abstracted and idealized Arabness; it is an Arabness that forms no more than one tendency in a panoramic, organic continuum of socio-cultural tendencies.

Furthermore, this process of African cultural metamorphosis did not stop with the advent of European colonialism. It continued in leaps and bounds to give the entire continent a new cultural complexity that was again incorporated into the identities of virtually all the African peoples, including the Swahili. Indeed, within a span of less than sixty years, Africans experienced a degree of cultural transfiguration that had no parallel in Asian countries, some of which experienced over two hundred years of European colonialism. Yet, interestingly enough, the European cultural tendency in Swahili identity, unlike its

Arab counterpart, has not been a cause of intellectual alarm that puts the Africanity of the Swahili in doubt. This only attests to the Eurocentric bias in the conception of Swahili identity.

From our presentation so far it should not be misunderstood that the Arab element had no input or was of marginal influence in Swahili identity. On the contrary, we believe that the Arab factor was *fundamentally* a part of the peopling of Swahililand. It can even be claimed that the Swahili started as a plural community on an Arab base. It was in a sense an Arab creole community of African origin. At no time, however, was the composition of this community static: it was always dynamic and growing. In due course it became ethnically "decreolized," so to speak, by absorbing other Africans into its organism as well as non-Africans, creating a multidimensional ethno-cultural continuum similar to the ones that have been evolving throughout the rest of Africa. These ethno-cultural continua are possible because the boundaries of group identity are always *fluid*. There is always that thin line where being a Hausa or a non-Hausa, being a Zulu or a non-Zulu, being a Swahili or a non-Swahili is arbitrary and artificial. If we can truly construct boundaries of ethnicity, then they are bound to be overlapping boundaries. Ethnic groups exist not necessarily because of cultural differentiation. Oftentimes they exist because the politics of the area in general, and the politics of disempowerment and marginalization in particular, force groups to assert a cultural distinctiveness that is sometimes largely imaginary.

That sense of distinctiveness is not maintained by a group once and for all. As group members interact among themselves in achieving the goals of the group, and as they interact with out-group members, their sense of group identity may either widen or narrow, it may intensify or decline, it may be more inclusive or more exclusive. But in general the more a population is "minoritized," the more it is refused recognition and membership into the larger society, the more assertive it may become about its ethnic identity.

We contend that a fresh look at Swahili identity must begin with a complete and total rejection of Northern models of human relations. It must reject the satatic quality, atomism, and inherent racism of Eurocentric paradigms of identity. It must reject the idea that a people's identity can be fossilized in time and subjected to a componential analysis with meticulous detachment from the substance of operation, rejecting some "components" while fetishing others.

In short, group identities are not determined by who we are genetically nor how we as *individuals* regard ourselves. They are, rather, dynamic conceptions of the collective self, constructed in time and place, both epistemologically and socially, in opposition to such other collective selves, always in the context of specific politico-economic conditions. It is for this reason that we once again want to assert that the Swahili are a *kabila*, clear and simple.

CHAPTER TWO:
LANGUAGE AND
SWAHILI IDENTITY

 identity of a people is often intimately related to their language. In the majority of non-European cases in the world, language still serves as one of the least problematic parameters by which a people can be defined.[12] As we indicated in the previous chapter, in both the Arab and African paradigms of identity, speaking a language as a native tongue is frequently a necessary and often a *sufficient* condition for group membership. As Edward Sapir once said, "a particular language tends to become the fitting expression of a self-conscious nationality and . . . such a group will construct for itself, in spite of all that physical anthropologists can do, a race to which is to be attributed the mystic power of creating a language and a culture as twin expressions of its psychic peculiarities" (29).[13] It is no wonder, then, that the struggles of nationalities for self-determination throughout the world are often accompanied by movements of linguistic assertion and rejuvenation.

In the case of the Swahili, however, the relationship between their identity and their language has tended to be complicated by several factors. Some of these have to do with etymological questions, some revolve around problems of linguistic formation and language classification, others are connected with the process of the spread and expansion of Swahili as such, and still others are concerned with what we may term "language attitudes" in the dual sense of peoples' attitudes towards a particular language or a variety thereof, and a peoples' attitudes towards other people on the basis of linguistic variance. In what follows we shall discuss the "problem" of a language-bound definition of the Swahili in light of these factors.

1. The Etymological Problem

The etymological level of the linguistic problem of Swahili identity concerns the very term "Swahili" by which the people are also known. It is often assumed that the term "Swahili" is foreign in origin and did not come into existence on the east African coast until well after the tenth century. It is granted, however, that the people may have existed before then; what they lacked was simply a Swahili identity. A "Swahili" collective consciousness, it is believed, could not have been forged before the term "Swahili" came into popular use. "Swahili," then, is not regarded to have developed into a full-fledged ethnonym until relatively recently.

The hypothesis that postulates a foreign origin for "Swahili" holds that the term is a derivative of the Arabic *Sawahil*. Though often translated as "coast" or "coastlands," Tolmacheva (1976) has shown quite convincingly that the term had multiple meanings in Arabic usage, including ports, port-towns, and harbors. If Swahililand has long included a chain of port-towns, then, it stands to reason that the Arabs began using the term *Sawahil* toponymically to refer to these east African ports. As usually happens throughout the world, the toponym eventually came to refer to the people, their language and their culture.

An alternative explanation traces the term to a local, Swahili origin, in particular to *siwa-hili* (literally "this island"). From this stem is derived *Wa-siwa-hili* (people of this island), *Ki-siwa-hili* (language of this island), and so forth in conformity with the affixation rules of the language. The Swahili are, after all, predominantly an island people, a people concentrated on a host of east African islands with only a fraction inhabiting sections of the mainland. This derivation would be in conformity with the Comoro usage of the term *Shi-ma-siwa* (literally "language of the islands") to refer to one of their dialects of Swahili. As might be expected, this and other explanations that stress a local origin of the term Swahili are espoused mainly by Swahili and other African nationalists in response to the Arab bias that is found in virtually every aspect of Swahili studies. How substantive each of these hypotheses is, however, has now become a matter of conjecture.

The first documentary evidence of a people calling themselves Swahili does not seem to appear until after the inception of British colonialism. In 1814, for example, Salt described his encounter with the people who called themselves "Sowahili." "This tribe," according to Salt, "dwells on the Eastern Coast of Africa, extending from Mugdasho . . . to the neighbourhood of Mombasa" (Appendix 1). But oral sources familiar with the "Chronicle of Pate" and other Swahili chronicles insist that, at least in the vicinity of the Lamu archepelago, the term was in use as early as the thirteenth century or even before.

Be that as it may, it seems to us that views on the origins of the term "Swahili" and the historical point at which it became an ethnonym is destined to remain largely speculative, given the nature (and paucity) of available evidence. What is important is to recognize that before the people became "Swahili," they existed as a set of interrelated communities identified mainly by their geographical locations. Thus the Swahili of Lamu, Mvita, Pemba, and Kilindini, for example, became Waamu, Wamvita, Wapemba, and Wakilindi, respectively. But somewhere between Arab rule and British colonialism a sense of wider Swahili identity emerged. Just as British colonialism in Nigeria was instrumental in forging a sense of wider Igbo identity, and just as British colonialism in Kenya triggered a sense of a wider Luhya or Mijikenda identity, it is reasonable to assume that colonialism on the east coast of Africa did much to prompt a wider sense of Swahili identity. In other words, the term Swahili and its exact origins are quite incidental to the broadening of the identity of the people. Colonialism would probably have created a consciousness of wider identity whatever the origins of the term. The debate on the origins and historicity of the term Swahili has so far been inadvertently informed by a linguistic philosophy that considers language as a determinant of thought and cognition, which holds that a notion, a concept, a consciousness cannot exist prior to its linguistic being. But we contend that language is a communication idiom and an expression of thought, so that if "Swahili" did not already exist as a term, the sense of a wider consciousness of identity that was generated by the politics of colonialism would in any case have found some other linguistic expression.

But the Swahili do not, of course, exist in a vacuum. They are part of an entire network of relations with other peoples. Swahili identity had to become "public knowledge," and it would not have become "public knowledge" without acquiring a linguistic label. Without such a label to communicate their self-conception, they would have had little social relevance, because there was no "knowledge" of their existence as a unit in the first place. The emergence of a social label thus carries with it the introduction of social identity to the sphere of "public knowledge." The issue, in other words, is not the terminological origin but the construction of a communicable, collective self-awareness.

2. Origins and Formations

The Eurocentric view of the Swahili people as a "racial mixture" has also been extended to their language. Just as the people are often regarded as offspring of African-Arab miscegenation, the language, too, has sometimes been seen by many nonlinguists as the product of "a love affair" between Arabic and the local languages of the east African coast. This correlation between the people and their language in terms of a "mixture" is well expressed in Madan's statement: "The term Swahili represents, ethnologically as well as linguistically, the mixture of African and Arab elements on the East Coast of Africa" (1903:v).

Thus an impression was created that without Arabic there would have been no Swahili language just as the concept of a Swahili people would have been impossible without the aid of "Arab blood." Swahili as a "hybrid" child of mixed parentage was in a sense part and parcel of that European fixation with "purity." Swahili, then, became an "impure" and, therefore, an inferior linguistic formation. As Wilfred Whiteley once noted, "It is not difficult to find views put forward that Swahili is somehow a hybrid of Arabic and a Bantu language, that it is somehow not a proper language, that it has 'no grammar' nor literature" (1969: 7-8). With a somewhat different emphasis, Mohamed Hyder observes that many people "have held the view believed to be originally from the Rev. Canon Hellier that Swahili is a hybrid language of Bantu and Arabic origin. The author does not share this view. . . . In biological terminology, one would say that the so called hybridization is not and never has been a genetic process which affects the form and structure of the language, but a phenotypic manifestation related to function" (81). Whatever the case, the idea that Swahili was no more than a bastard, hybrid child of an unholy African-Arab union had now received the sacred seal of the scholarly word and was bound to influence future generations, for better or for worse.

Initially the conception of the Swahili language as an African-Arab mixture of a sort may not have been unrelated to the colonial politics of the time. As we have learnt from the African colonial experience in general, colonial military invasions and subsequent rule were often preceded by a series of Christian missionary ventures. Christian missionary enterprises were almost indispensable in laying the ideological foundations of colonialism. As mentioned earlier, the civilizing mission was initially based on the Europeanization of Christianity, on the myth that Christianity was European and Euro-Christians themselves were the bearers of human civilization. Before administrative colonialism could be securely established, therefore, the primitivity and barbarity of the "native" had to be tamed by the divine power of the gospel. The education of the "native" was thus inseparable from the attempted Christian saving of "heathen" souls.

But communication with the indigenous population proved problematic to the missionary establishment. The "natives" were not familiar with European languages, and the Christian initiation of the population through the spiritual transportation of Jesus to the "dark continent" could certainly not be made to wait until the African had acquired a foreign language. The solution was to get the bearers of the biblical word to learn the languages of the Africans, a linguistic task that they assumed with characteristic missionary zeal. One of the results of this policy was the codification of several African languages, i.e., their reduction to writing in the Latin script and some degree of standardization.

This linguistic policy of the missionary establishment, however, did not always solve the problem of spiritual communication. Apart from the question of which language or set of languages to select for missionary work from the multitude of African languages, there was the consideration of what language would be most effective in spreading the Christian word. A section of missionaries, inspired by David Livingstone, believed that the best way of reaching the African spiritually was through his "tribal" milieu and medium. Missionary acquisition of all and every possible African language, therefore, was encouraged, again as a matter of policy.

Other missionaries, however, were highly suspicious of many of the African languages. They feared that a majority of these languages were so infused with idolatrous and animistic concepts that their use in African Christianity was bound to corrupt the Christian message. To these missionaries only European languages could impart the true Christian message; and if Christianity was to be truly consummated in Africa, there was no satisfactory alternative but to teach European languages. But, then, God could not be made to wait, hence an interim linguistic arrangement had to be forged. It was a section of these missionaries who became inclined towards Swahili, which, in their opinion, had virtually lost its "idolatrous" and "animistic" content due to its long exposure to the outside world and to monotheism. The fact that Swahili was already a language of wider communication added to its credentials, and soon Swahili was to become the major language of east African Christianity. Just as Swahili came to aid the spread of the Christian church, the church in turn came to aid the further spread of Swahili.

Swahili as a language of Christianity, however, was not without its adversaries. There was a section of the missionaries that was suspicious of the kind of monotheism supposedly inherent in the Swahili language. To these missionaries the monotheistic content of Swahili was essentially Islamic, hence a monotheism they found wholly objectionable and antithetical to Christianity. They sustained this argument by pointing to the Arabic elements in Swahili. Capitalizing on the Eurocentric equation that Islam was as Arab as Christianity was European, they argued that Arabisms in Swahili necessarily carried the substance and spirit of Islam. To these people, then, the "Arabness" of Swahili discredited it as a possible language of Christianity; and so the Christian campaign against Islam was also extended to the Swahili language.[14]

This tendency to associate Swahili with Islam was by no

means restricted to Kenya. In German East Africa, or what was later to become Tanganyika, the same fears were expressed. Wright, for example, notes:

> In Germany, Director Buchner proved to be an unrelenting foe of Swahili, going so far in a speech before the Kolonialrat in 1905 as to declare that it was so irredeemably mixed with Islam that every expedient ought to be employed to obstruct their joint penetration. . . . Buchner's opposition to Swahili was adopted and expanded by Julius Richter, a member of the Berlin Committee. Richter delivered a diatribe during the Kolonial Kongress in 1905 against the pernicious influence of Islam everywhere in Africa. Isolating East Africa as the scene of the worst danger, he envisaged a mosque alongside every coastman's hut, and took the official support for Swahili to be blatantly pro-Islamic. (1971:113)

Naturally this fear of Islam led to the tendency to give undue prominence to the Arabness of the Swahili language and, as we demonstrated in the previous chapter, of the Swahili people. The Arab bias thus came to obfuscate not only the origin and identity of the people, but also their linguistic definition as a people.

The more advanced methods of linguistic science, in contrast to those of ethnography, however, soon came to challenge the idea that Swahili is a pro-Islamic language and a linguistic hybrid. The respected German linguist Carl Meinhof alleviated Christian fears by suggesting that Swahili could be Christianized, and that missions should take the initiative to do so (Wright, 1971:113). Descriptive and historical linguists were soon able to prove that the language was African, and specifically "Bantu," in form and origin; and that its supposed Arabness was no more than a product of lexical borrowing that is no more a unique attribute of Swahili than it is of any other language in the world.

In this connection the most extensive study is perhaps that of Nurse and Spear (1985), in which they classify Swahili as a Sabaki language belonging, with many other languages like Pokomo, Zigula, Pare, and Zaramo, to the Northeastern Coast Group of the Eastern Bantu Family. Descriptive linguistics has also demonstrated that Swahili, like virtually any other language, is divided into several regional dialects like Chimiini, Kibajuni, Kisiu, Kipate, Kiamu, Kimvita, Kivumba, Kipemba, Kiunguja, and so forth, all of which are, to one degree or another, mutually intelligible.

Expectedly, it is the modern linguistic position that Swahili nationalists[15] came to espouse. If the ethnographic Eurocentric scholarship tended to overplay the Arabness of the language, Swahili nationalists now came to overplay its Bantuness. The Eurocentric tendency to *over-Arabize* the Swahili language now came to be confronted with a Swahili nationalist inclination to *de-Arabize* it. We have sometimes come across Swahili nationalists who claim that it is, in fact, possible to speak or write a Swahili that is free of Arabic-loaned words. In their reaction, therefore, the Swahili nationalists seem to have been infected with the Eurocentric bug of "purism."

In addition to establishing the Bantu origins of Swahili, linguistics also tried, less successfully perhaps, to put a date on its historical point of emergence as an independent language. The idea is that there existed a hypothetical (reconstructed) parent language, so to speak, which, together with other hypothetical "parents" and hypothetical "grandparents," belonging to a hypothetical family of eastern Bantu languages. These hypothetical linguistic parents, or proto-languages as linguists would call them, were more like amoebas than humans. The amoeba would reproduce essentially by splitting into two. Each of these parts would now have a life of its own, grow, and eventually reproduce, again by splitting into two. The same principle applies to linguistic reproduction, and a language is said to have come into being at the point at which its parent splits into two or more independent languages.

For historical linguists, then, the task was one of determining at exactly what point Swahili, Pokomo, Mijikenda, and so forth separated from a hypothetical umbrella Sabaki parent to become independent languages. According to Ohly (1973) the language originated sometime before the tenth century. Somewhat in agreement with Ohly, Nurse and Spear place the birth of Swahili sometime after A.D. 500 and proceed to suggest that by the ninth century "an early form of Swahili was probably spoken in these coastal settlements, not merely in the north but at least as far south as Kilwa" (49).

Swahili nationalists, however, are bothered by this Eurocentric tendency to ignore oral sources from the traditions of the Swahili society itself in connection with the history of their language — and of course their people. To them, this is tantamount to European appropriation of Swahili history. Chiraghdin (1974), for example, recounts the local version of the history of the Swahili language as having originated from a preexisting Kingozi supposedly spoken at one time in and around the Lamu archepelago on the northern coast of Kenya. Using arguments based on observations contained in the second century document, *The Periplus of the Erythaean Sea*, Chiraghdin further suggests that there is no reason to believe that "Swahili" could not in fact have existed prior to the second century of the Christian era.

Chiraghdin's arguments are certainly not based on any scientific data; they are merely based on scientific reasoning. But what is important is that these sentiments were expressed at a time when there was mounting danger of Swahili disenfranchisement. Under such political circumstances a rejection of the Swahili version of the history of their language could easily translate into a rejection of the historicity of the people themselves. And to suggest that Swahili came into being at some vague moment before the tenth century was, in a sense, to question the temporal depth of Swahili history. Chiraghdin's position, then, was an expression of a Swahili nationalist posture in a neocolonialist period that was, and continues to be, rife with the politics of disempowerment of certain classes and certain nationalities.

To provide this political qualification to Chiraghdin's views, however, does not mean that he is altogether wrong. Raymond Ohly inadvertently raises an interesting paradox in connection with the term Swahili: "It is still impossible to establish which was the first ethnic Bantu group referred to under the common name Swahili" (483, n. 1). Ohly definitely accepts the idea that Swahili emerged through a process of differentiation from a parent Sabaki language, or proto-Sabaki. But languages do not differentiate from their "parents" in a vacuum; they do so with a social group of speakers. The question, then, is what were these people and their language called at the point of differentiation from its Sabaki parents? Could these supposedly Bantu people and their language have gone by the name "Ngozi" as suggested by Chiraghdin on the basis of the Swahili oral tradition? In other words, could "Ngozi" have been the proto-Swahili that differentiated into separate linguistic-cum-geographical groups all along the coast, groups that only much later developed a sense of ethnic oneness?

If one does not attribute the origins of the Swahili language to proto-Bantu, on the other hand, it is Chiraghdin's sentiments about the age of the language that may have strong elements of truth in it. The problem with linguistic reconstruction as a method of tracing the origins of languages is that it makes allowance for only one process of language formation, the process by which hypothetical parent languages break up into two or more linguistic siblings (which are at the same time potentially new linguistic parents). But, of course, this is not the only means by which languages come into being. Important for our purposes is the linguistic process that begins with a *pidgin*, which may become a *creole* and may end with a phenomenon that linguists call *decreolization*. Let us now look at what all this really means.

A pidgin is essentially an auxiliary language that develops to fulfill a narrow range of linguistic functions. It arises in a situation in which there are several linguistic groups of people who need to communicate with each other for reasons of trade, for example, but lack a common medium of communication. Precisely because of its limited functions that usually do not involve expression of abstract and/or complex thought, a pidgin would normally have a small range of vocabulary drawn, to a very large extent, from one language. Its grammatical structure would also be somewhat "simpler" and would be based, to a large extent, on some universal features of the grammar of human languages.

In time a pidgin may acquire extended functions as areas of interaction between peoples from different linguistic groups increase. Slavery, the emergence of new administrative structures in a community, a high incidence of intermarriages among ethnic groups are some examples of the human experience which could diversify the functions of a pidgin. This functional diversification of a pidgin not seldom leads to its gradual acquisition as a first, and sometimes the only, language by a significant group of people. Eventually it may become a first language to members of an entire society. Once this happens, once a pidgin becomes the first language of a speech community, then it is said to have become a creole. There is evidence, for example, that what is today called Nigerian Pidgin is already becoming a creole as an increasing number of Nigerian children are growing up speaking Nigerian Pidgin as their first or only language.

The central difference, then, between a pidgin and a creole is that the latter has what we may call native speakers, while the former does not. The vocabulary and structure of a pidgin are generally carried over into a creole. But because a creole is expected to perform many more functions than a pidgin it gradually acquires an expanded lexicon and a more elaborate grammar. In such cases, the substratum languages, the languages that exist within the immediate environment of the creole, become the main source of its elaborated lexicon and grammatical system. In lexicon, however, a creole, like any other language, may continue to borrow from various other sources.

This process may not stop here. A creole may now be decreolized. It may draw more and more from its substratum languages to eventually acquire all the features, all the complexities, the depth and breadth of the "average human language." In essence, a decreolized language will have lost virtually all traces of its pidgin and creole genesis. And it is in connection with this process that linguistic reconstruction as a historical method is likely to fail. The chances are that historical linguistic reconstruction and the comparative method would trace the decreolized language to the same origins as one or more of the languages of the substratum.

But how does all this relate to the Swahili language specifically? As early as A.D. 100, the anonymous Greek author of *The Periplus of the Erythraean Sea*, who had travelled to east Africa, could already talk of Arabs who frequented the region for purposes of trade with "mainlanders of all the places" who, it is reasonable to assume, were from different linguistic backgrounds. Sociolinguists would agree that this socio-economic configuration meets the ideal description of a situation from which a pidgin could emerge. This anonymous Greek goes further by suggesting that these Arabs knew "the language of these people." The assumptions of this statement are (1) that the peoples of the area were *not* Arabs, (2) that they spoke a language that was not Arabic, and (3) that the Arab visitors were able to communicate with them in that language.[16]

The ease with which the Arab visitors acquired the supposed common language of this region, according to the impressions of the author of the *Periplus*, suggests that this language might in fact have been an auxiliary trade language, a pidgin; and given the commercial nature of the contact between the Arabs and peoples of the east African coast, it is not unreasonable to assume that it was a pidgin of Arabic, i.e., a pidgin whose vocabulary was heavily drawn from Arabic. On present evidence, the only language that is spoken in "all the places" throughout much of the east African coast, which also has a high proportion of vocabulary items of Arabic origin, is, of course, Swahili. If the author of the *Periplus* was correct in his or her impressions, therefore, the set of socio-economic and sociolinguistic considerations make it quite feasible that by A.D. 100 Swahili may already have been in formation, existing as a trade language or a pidgin during this early phase of its development.

If there were sufficient conditions for the evolution of a pidgin on the east coast of Africa by the first century of the Christian era, what could have prompted its development into a creole? The anonymous Greek author of the *Periplus* again provides us with an answer. Not only were the Arabs trading with the "mainlanders of all the places" throughout the coast, they were also intermarrying with them. The offspring of such intermarriages could then have acquired the pidgin language as their first and probably only tongue, raising the pidgin to the status of a creole. This process would be comparable to the situation in Africa today, where the offspring of African inter-ethnic marriages may end up speaking English, for example, as their first language. This shift from pidgin to creole on the east coast of Africa may again have occurred around, before, or after A.D. 100.

Once it became native to a substantial population of coastalists, the decreolization of the language could now begin. Capitalizing on the lexical and especially grammatical resources of its substratum languages, the creole became more and more like one or more of its surrounding languages, more and more like Pokomo and Mijikenda languages. It is in the continuation of this complex linguistic process that what is now called Swahili may have found its present form.

What evidence then can we provide to support such a hypothesis about the genesis of Swahili? A comparative study of pidgins and creoles would undoubtedly show that, from the descriptions presented by the author of the *Periplus* and subsequent writers among early travellers, the socio-economic circumstances of the ancient societies of the east African coast constituted a potential crucible for the organic evolution of a pidgin and creole language. Partly because the process of decreolization tends to obliterate the peculiar features of pidgins and creoles, however, linguistic evidence for this Swahili genesis is not easy to find. But the hypothesis would certainly explain Swahili's substantial proportion of Arabic words, its lack of a tonal system that is characteristic of virtually all other neighboring African languages, and the fewer distinctions in its concord system.

Clearly, then, our views are somewhat in accord with those of early European ethnographers insofar as we regard both Arabic and Bantu languages as instrumental in the formation of Swahili. Today Swahili is classified as a Bantu language less because of its vocabulary, but more because of its grammatical structure. As we have suggested already, while the pidginization of Swahili may have relied almost exclusively on an Arabic lexicon, its grammar was based predominantly on primary, universal patterns, not on Arabic grammar. This is probably why there is still overwhelming evidence of an Arabic lexicon but no evidence of Arabic grammatical patterns in contemporary Swahili. From its pidgin base, according to our hypothesis, the language creolized and decreolized in the direction of Bantu languages in structural and lexical terms, even though it probably continued to borrow lexically from Arabic as well as from other languages, both local and foreign.

Where we differ with the Eurocentric ethnographic scholarship concerning the genesis of Swahili, then, is in our understanding of the linguistic process by which the language came into being. The "ethnolinguists" based their views on the existence of many words of Arabic origin in the language, a phenomenon that could be explained, as linguists now do, by the rather universal phenomenon of "lexical borrowing." In addition, the ethnolinguists remained unclear about the nature of that putative linguistic mixture in the origins of Swahili. This created the conditions for the application of essentially racist notions like "bastard" and "hybrid" to an otherwise natural process of linguistic formation that may, in fact, explain the evolution of many languages throughout the world.

In addition, as we shall show further on, there has been the recurrent suggestion that because of the Arabic factor in its lexicon, Swahili is somehow less African than say the Luo, Kikuyu, or Turkana languages. As intimated in our Introduction, we find this position untenable, not only because Swahili was born in Africa and came to "maturation" as an organic linguistic product of the African experience, but also because Arabic is an African language. Demographically there are more speakers of Arabic as a first language, and, linguistically, there are more languages of the Semitic family, to which Arabic belongs, in Africa than in other parts of the world.

There is, of course, nothing wrong with recognizing Swahili's dual heritage. But we contend that Swahili's links with Arabic have become a fixation that has often led to doubts about its African credentials due to the Eurocentric tendency to de-Africanize the Arabic language. The fixation with Swahili's Arabic connections and the treatment of Arabic as non-African has understandably led to a nationalist reaction that now seeks to de-Arabize Swahili. Like the Swahili people, therefore, this complex linguistic organism of the African soil has been entrapped in a Eurocentric racial equation that posits a "two-nature theory" of the language, polarized between its supposed Arabness and supposed Africanness. Arabic is said to belong to the "Arab race." "African languages" are said to belong to an "African race," and by implication, Swahili, because of its dual "nature," is seen as "sui generis, neither Arab nor African." The old Eurocentric, anthropological fallacy that equated language with race on a global scale, therefore, now came to bedevil the linguistic world of the Swahili people on a more local scale.

To conclude this section, it may be an interesting twist of fate that the language that arose from pidgin origins may itself be giving birth to a pidgin formation of a sort. There is evidence that the long interaction of the coastal Swahili people with a variety of inland people has given rise to what Bernd Heine calls Kenya Pidgin-Swahili (1973). And it is probably in connection with this emergent variety of Pidgin-Swahili that J. W. T. Allen once observed:

> The efforts required of an African to learn to speak Swahili up to an adequate level is negligible and is comparable with the effort required of English and French schoolchildren who are required to learn and speak `standard' at school, whilst speaking dialect at home. Most Africans totally ignorant of Swahili, will in six weeks or less, pick up a knowledge of it sufficient to enable them to carry on a conversation about any of the normal affairs of life. It is a curious fact that it appears to make little difference whether the mother tongue is Bantu or non-Bantu. (1959: 71-2)

It is in the nature of pidgins that they are acquired relatively fast. And the fact that both Bantu and non-Bantu peoples would acquire a pidgin of Swahili with equal speed perhaps attests to a pidgin's basic, structurally universalist tendencies. Will this Kenya pidgin-Swahili someday become creolized and, ultimately, decreolized into yet another African language? This possibility perhaps militated against the concerted school and media efforts to promote standard Swahili throughout the society.

3. Spread and Expansion

At one time the Swahili people could easily have been defined as those to whom Swahili was a first or native language. However, the distortion that "there is no such thing as Swahili tribe" (to use the Kenya Ministry of Tourism's dictum) naturally led to the conclusion that Swahili belonged to no specific group, that it had no ethnic base. This popular conception, in other words, made the language-ethnicity equation in connection with the Swahili increasingly difficult in the minds of out-group members. Also, the fact that the Swahili are today a small, almost invisible, demographic minority, while their language has spread far and wide out of proportion to the size of its population, only intensifies the view that Swahili is no man's language, a language of all and of none at the same time.

The spread of Swahili beyond its narrow coastal origins may

have started with Swahili participation, with people of other origins, in the once flourishing Indian Ocean trade. A variety of commodities that were in demand in other parts of the world were brought to the coast from the hinterland by peoples of the African interior (Chittick, 108-09). These "commodities" included slaves. Like other African groups in both east and west Africa, some members of the Swahili community were lured by profit and greed to negate their humanity and contribute to the cruel bondage of others. The international economics of one facet of this east African experience are well laid out by Abdul Sheriff (1987) in his rigorous study of *Slaves, Spices and Ivory in Zanzibar*. This trade may have served as the initial impetus to the spread of Swahili as deeply into the continent as the Zaire of today.

The economic foundations that contributed to the spread of the Swahili language did not, of course, come to an end with the decline of the Indian Ocean trade. Capitalism brought home new forms of internal trade and commerce, new forms of economic interaction, new and multitiered forms of economic linkages that have continued to expand Swahili's demographic horizons. From the local marketplace in small towns to the production spots of the manufacturing industry to international trade between nations like Kenya and Tanzania, African economics has continued to affect the destiny of the Swahili language.

The economic enterprise in connection with the spread of Swahili was followed by the missionary enterprise. As indicated earlier, many European missionaries who came to open up the way for colonialism, to pioneer the "divine" cause of European imperialism, were forced to learn Swahili and use it in their evangelist mission. Because of their need for it, they were forced to codify the language, use it in the translation of the Bible and Christian hymns, and impart it to their African flocks. Swahili also came to be taught, sometimes intensively, in some Christian missionary schools, adding a new dimension to its spread and development. The missionary force was, of course, ultimately taken over by Africans themselves, bringing the language even closer to the laity and extending its roots deep into sections of east African Christianity. The Salvation Army, for example, has played and continues to play a major role in the popularization of Swahili. Again, like the economic institution, the Christian institution has continued to break down walls which had hitherto confined the expansion and internationalization of Swahili in Africa.

The missionary establishment, having fulfilled its divine mission of providing access to European colonialism, now had to share the platform with the colonial administration in determining the social flow of the Swahili language. In German Tanganyika, the case was somewhat clearer and more consistent. The German colonial administrators, partly guided by the view that no African deserved to acquire the German language, partly by pragmatic considerations, and partly by concerns to limit African cultural disruptions, were quick to adopt a policy that favored the use of the already widely spread Swahili language in the lower levels of its administration. The German colonial administration thus designed a Swahili curriculum for government schools. Initially, as we noted above, there were pockets of resistance from sections of the missionary establishment to this policy due mainly to Swahili's association with Islam. Nonetheless Swahili's official status, its participation in the affairs of the state, became one additional motive for its acquisition and use by Africans of various backgrounds.

The British colonial policy towards Swahili was somewhat more eclectic. We have already commented on the different factional interests within the British Christian missionary establishment around the question of Swahili's role in church affairs. This is one area that required the mediation of the British colonial administration. But this administration also had to confront the more assertive linguistic interests of British colonial settlers. These settlers needed cheap labor for their plantations, which they were willing to recruit from any and all ethnic groups. The same applied to British factories. The British settlers, then, favored the promotion of the transethnic Swahili language that could expedite the proletarianization of the African. They were not in favor of promoting other African languages, which they viewed as so localized as to impede the social unification of their labor pool; English, in their opinion, would only make Africans cheeky.

In addition to the missionary and settler domains, the British colonial administration had its own specific interests in a

Swahili policy. Like the Germans in Tanganyika, the British needed Africans in their lower administrative structures. But precisely because they had selected English as the official medium of administration, there was a need to produce African functionaries adequately tutored in the English language and to some extent English mannerisms. It is in trying to accommodate the interests of these forces that the British colonial government in east Africa ended up with a rather inconsistent language policy. Nonetheless, the overall effect was still in favor of the continued spread of the Swahili language.

The neocolonial state in east Africa has also played its part in the spread of the Swahili language. In Tanzania, Swahili has been the national and official language of the country since the 1960s, strengthening its use in all areas of Tanzanian life from the domestic to the state. In Kenya, too, Swahili has been the national language since the 1970s and has now become a compulsory subject throughout elementary and secondary education. In Uganda, Swahili became the national language in the 1970s and more recently became the official language of the National Resistance Army, so that its use is constantly expanding. The school, the written media, the radio, and the television, which have evolved since the colonial days as adjuncts of the nation-state, have all combined to create more and more space for the demographic expansion of Swahili.

This historical development of Swahili has given rise to new varieties of the language that are gradually becoming native to an increasing number of east Africans. The concept of a "Swahili-speaking" people, therefore, has now transcended Swahili ethnicity in the narrower sense of the term, even though it fits perfectly well with the Swahili multidimensional concept of *kabila*. This then has created a complex situation of new public affirmations and counter-affirmations about the boundaries of Swahili identity.

The process of Swahili's standardization is of particular significance in this regard. Once the British recognized the need to use Swahili in some of their spheres of interaction with the "native," it became necessary to establish one pan-dialect, to select, from the numerous dialects that existed on the coast as well as in the interior of east Africa, one dialect upon which a "standard" Swahili could be founded. For a host of historical and politico-economic reasons that we need not go into here, Kiunguja, the Swahili dialect of Zanzibar, was finally selected for this purpose. Henceforth orthographization, structural systematization, lexical expansion, and other linguistic efforts at "creating" a standard norm revolved essentially around Kiunguja. The result was a standard Swahili based on Kiunguja, but at the same time paradoxically different from it. And it certainly could not have been, nor need it have been, otherwise.

It is in the Swahili response, however, that we discover the real significance of the spread and standardization of the Swahili language for the question of Swahili identity. Probably the earliest documented Swahili response came from Sheikh Al-Amin Ali Mazrui (1931), the distinguished Muslim scholar from Mombasa, who complained that the Latin script adopted for (standard) Swahili and used in schools was inadequate, that it distorted the phonetics of the Swahili language. To him the orthographic Latinization of Swahili constituted a violation of sophisticated Swahili speech, and he feared that the continued use of this orthography in schools was bound to eventually contort the speech of future generations of the Swahili. Using his reputedly fiery Kimvita paper *Al-Islah*, he urged his community to boycott this kind of Swahili. While Sheikh Al-Amin Ali Mazrui framed the issue in terms of orthography, the gist of his argument seemed to be that there was a definable Swahili phonetics that was now being threatened by the new, written version of "school Swahili."

Sentiments similar to those of Sheikh Al-Amin Ali Mazrui were raised again, over forty years later, by the vocal Swahili nationalist, Shihabuddin Chiraghdin. After discussing some of the problems he encountered with standard Swahili, Chiraghdin continued:

> Jambo jengine ambalo watu wengi hawalitaamali ni kuwa maandishi ya Kiswahili yaliyokuja yakaondolewa na Wazungu kwa kutumia herufi zao si maandishi ya Kiarabu: ni maandishi ya Kiswahili. Yaani katika taaluma za Kiswahili, Waswahili wenyewe walizichukua hati za Kiarabu na kuzitengeza ili ziweze kuandika lugha yao . . . [lakini] Wazungu walipotumia hati zao hawakuzirakibisha kulingana na sauti za Kiswahili. Kwa mfano, ukisoma "taa"

hujui ni ile itoayo mwangaza au ni samaki wa pwani. *Kurakibisha kwao ilikuwa ni kupotoa.* Badala ya "hikima," "ilimu" tukaambiwa ni "hekima" na "elimu," kwa maana kwa Wazungu "e" kwao ni "i." Kama waliachiwa wenyewe Waswahili wangeweza kuzirakibisha hata hati hizo za Kiswahili. (1974:16)

Another thing which many people do not comprehend is that the Swahili orthography, which Europeans replaced with their own script was, in fact, not Arabic orthography: it was Swahili. In Swahili education, the Swahili took the Arabic script and modified it so it could express the sounds of their language. . . [But] when Europeans used their script they did not modify it to reflect the phonetics of the Swahili language. For example, when you read the word "taa" you do not know whether it is that which emits light [a lamp] or a fish [mantaray]. Their adjustment was, in fact, distortion. Instead of "hikima" "ilimu," etc. we now had "hekima" and "elimu" because for the Europeans "e" is "i." If the development of the orthography (using the Roman alphabet) was left to the Swahili themselves they would have been able to reflect Swahili sounds more correctly.

Chiraghdin then ends with an urgent note that, while he was in sympathy with the idea of a standard Swahili, the standard version bequeathed to us by British colonialism should not be swallowed "line, hook and sinker" (1974:17), nor accepted without some serious reservations.

We can appreciate Sheikh Al-Amin Mazrui's and Chiraghdin's position more fully when we consider the extent to which Europeans were involved in setting the written norm of standard Swahili in its early years of evolution. According to Jack D. Rollins:

In terms of literary influence, one set of figures alone will explain more than several paragraphs. Between the years 1900-1950, there were approximately 359 works of prose published in Swahili; 346 of these were written by Europeans and published mainly in England and Germany. Many of these were translations: Swift, Bunyan, Moliere, Shakespeare, but none more pervasive, in more abundance, and having more effect than the Bible. The British and Foreign Bible Society Archives in London show that thousands of copies of either books from the Bible, or the entire Bible itself, had been distributed in East Africa by the turn of the century. A common yearly run was between 5-10,000 copies. This is not to mention the many editions of individual hymn books, catechisms, prayer books, lives of saints and so on that also quickly found their way into Swahili by the beginning of the 20th century. (51)

In his statistics Rollins certainly could not have included works published by Muslim scholars like Sheikh Al-Amin Ali Mazrui or Sheikh Abdulla Saleh Farsy. Nonetheless, the overwhelming proportion of widely circulating, Euro-Christian-produced materials, using what they conceived to be standard Swahili, thus came to be the linguistic ideal by which east Africans, including the Swahili people themselves, were now expected to abide.

The final example of Swahili response to standard Swahili and the relatively more recent varieties that have emerged with the spread of the language into the interior is offered by the Kenya Swahili Council (*Baraza la Kiswahili Kenya*). This is a non-governmental organization that was formed in Mombasa, Kenya, sometime in the 1970s under the name *Jungu Kuu*, with the explicit objective of putting Kenya at the front line of developing the Swahili language. It was felt that, though Kenya is the "birth place" of Swahili, the brunt of the responsibility in the development of the language has been left to neighboring Tanzania.

But the predominantly Swahili composition of the *Baraza's* executive staff also betrays a purist motive, a Swahili nationalist motive that seeks to keep the language of their identity "authentic." For example, in the first issue of *Mwangaza wa Lugha*, a publication of the Swahili Council, there is a whole column entitled "Nyosha Kiswahili Chako" (literally "Straighten Your Swahili") by Hassan Msami, whose stated objective is:

. . . Kutoa mafunzo ya lugha safi, kwa wale wananchi ambao hutumia vibaya baadhi ya maneno ya lugha hii.

Katika safu hii tutakuwa tukiwakosoa na kuwapa mwon-
gozo wale wote wasioelewa kutamka vyema maneno fulani
fulani ya Kiswahili. . . . (15)

. . . to provide lessons of pure language to those nationals
who use some words of this language inappropriately.

In this column we will [also] correct and give guidance to
all those who do not understand the correct pronunciation
of certain Swahili words. . . .

Clearly, then, there is an element of linguistic purity that
informs the work of the council, inspired by the fear that if the
Swahili people themselves do not intervene at this critical historical moment, their language will be mismanaged or dragged
into the linguistic gutters, so to speak. So in the same column,
commenting on the alarming rate at which the word *posho* has
been semantically distorted, for example, the writer remarks:

. . . sasa upotoshi huo umeanza kupiga hatua kubwa na
hata hivi sasa umefikia kiwango cha hatari cha kuanza
kuzoweleka kwa kuonekana kuwa ni msemo tu wa
kawaida ulio sahihi ambao Waswahili hutumia katika
msamiati wao. (Msami:15)

. . . now this distortion has begun to gain much ground
and has reached the dangerous point of being habitually
regarded as normal and as the correct way of using the word
in the assumption that the Swahili people themselves use in
their vocabulary.

The same fears have also been expressed in connection with
the attempt to expand the Swahili lexicon to meet the demands
of the technological and scientific age. While members of the
Baraza la Kiswahili, or what was then *Jungu Kuu*, commended
Tanzania's efforts in this regard, they felt that Tanzanian language planners were also *"unconsciously spoiling the language*
by adopting words from other languages or writing them reck-
lessly whilst the words are already in existence in many
[Swahili] dialects" (Nabhany and Kamal Khan, 1978:6).

It would be wrong, however, to regard all these sentiments of
Swahili scholars as no more than idealistic yearnings for a

"pure" Swahili. These sentiments are also indirect affirmations of their sense of being, of how they view the linguistic boundaries of their identity. They are indications that, despite their dialectal differences, they are conscious of a certain common denominator which defines their ethnicity. There is no doubt that this consciousness is based on rather shaky linguistic grounds; though in a sense, that is the story of ethnicity the world over.

But one could perhaps explain this phenomenon by invoking the notion of "primary dialects." With regard to Swahili this would include all the dialects that existed before the spread of the language into the interior and the rise of a standard Swahili. In essence these are the regional dialects by which various Swahili groups used to define themselves. These would include Chimiini in Somalia; Kisiu, Kipate, Kiamu, Kimvita, Chichifundi, Kivumba in Kenya; Kimtang'ata, Kipemba, Kitumbatu, Kihadimu, Kiunguja, Kimakunduchi in Tanzania; Kimgao and Kimwani in Mozambique; Kingazija, Kimwali, Shinziwani, Kimaote in the Comoro Islands. A Swahili person defined in such terms would in fact be in conformity with the dictionary definition of *Kamusi ya Kiswahili Sanifu* as "mtu asiyekuwa na lugha nyingine yoyote ya jadi yake isipokuwa Kiswahili — "a person with no other language of his tradition except Swahili." "Traditional" Swahili in this sense can be considered equivalent, at this historical juncture, to Swahili's primary dialects.

In a sense, then, these purist sentiments of the Swahili scholars are perhaps subconscious efforts to redefine the linguistic boundaries of Swahili identity. In view of the neocolonial politics of the region that are wont to breed ethnic sentiments, they have sensed a need to qualify the linguistic definition of a Swahili. They are in a sense saying that a person does not become Swahili merely by speaking just any variety of the language. To qualify for Swahili identity one has to acquire, as a first language, an in-group variety of the language, a Swahili of the Swahili people themselves. The struggle here, then, is to make sure that those who become Swahili through linguistic assimilation do so on the terms of the Swahili people themselves and not on the linguistic terms established by forces created by east Africa's colonial and neocolonial regimes. We may even go further to claim that had the Swahili people felt more politically secure within east Africa's borders, had they felt no threat of political and economic disenfranchisement, they would have probably been more flexible on the linguistic definition of ethnicity. But the fact of the matter is that they do feel the threat of marginalization, and that threat, as we shall show in our conclusion, is not imaginary. It is very real. The struggle for the self-preservation of the Swahili community, therefore, would naturally include tendencies that assert their linguistic, cultural, religious distinctiveness.

4. Language Attitudes

We may define language attitudes as the subjective, psycho-social reactions to the language itself, or some of its inherent qualities, or towards the people who speak that language. In what follows we shall attempt to look at language attitudes because we believe that this mode of stereotyping, if we may call it so, can become important in the struggles for definition and redefinition of identities.

Despite the fact that the science of linguistics has long proved otherwise, the view that Swahili is a "bastard" language has persisted to this day. This view, however, did not remain at the level of conception; it was ultimately socialized into an attitude that has affected people's responses towards the language. As a result of this attitude, for example, Whiteley reports that "in 1952 we find a reputable novelist declaring in one of those characteristically cosy after-dinner speeches that Swahili was a . . . `linguistic obscenity' to which no Briton `worth his salt' should be a part" (1969:7-8).

This sentiment essentially reflected the position of British settlers (in contrast to British administrators) as a ruling class in east Africa. Like all ruling classes the British settlers, while keen to see Swahili promoted as the language of labor, were wary of attempts to "make" it a language of "sophisticated" cultural expression, of a large body of literature and the arts. The consensus of opinion was that only English, their language, had the character and the right to assume a cultural supremacy in their colonial dominions. Even if Swahili was taught in primary schools, therefore, it was to be taught only as a way of producing a transethnic proletariat, as a linguistic preparation for the maximal exploitation of African labor.

The British settlers did, of course, use Swahili. Indeed, they used it so much that an entire variety of British settler Swahili, the so-called *Kisetla*, emerged. This became the language for the mobilization and supervision of African labor. But it also became the language by which the British could maintain some distance between themselves and the African. An African inter-locutor with a British settler may have been more conversant with the English language than the settler was with Swahili. But even in such circumstances the British settler would insist on speaking Swahili to the African. Such situations revealed not only the settler attitudes towards their African interlocutors as different and inferior, but also their attitudes towards the Swahili language as one belonging to an inferior people and useful only in putting the Africans in their place, economically and politically.

The same sentiments were later to be expressed, though per-haps in a more polite language, in the neocolonial era in Kenya. This was perhaps most clearly dramatized in a 1969 Kenya par-liamentary motion to introduce Swahili as the national lan-guage of the country and a medium of parliamentary discourse. The opposition to the language from supposedly enlightened Kenyan politicians literally shocked the average Kenyan. In the tradition of colonial ideology, Swahili was discredited as a hybrid child of Arab-Islamic origins unworthy of a national sta-tus and one that could not be expected to be the esteemed lan-guage by which the "honorable" members of parliament should be required to deliberate "serious" legislative matters of the nation. To cap it all, Charles Njonjo, the then-attorney general of the country and a politician of immense influence, declared that, in fact, Swahili is just as foreign to Kenya as the English language. Similar sentiments were, of course, expressed by other parliamentarians (Marshad, 1984:74).

Njonjo's Swahili-English equation essentially implied that the Swahili people, the native speakers of the Swahili language, were as foreign to Kenya as the English people who, barely six years before, were still riding, though not as firmly as before, on Kenya's colonial saddle. And just as the English were "kicked out," there was no reason why the Swahili could not, in principle, experience the same fate. Njonjo was, of course, well known in Kenya for his venomous aversion towards Arabs, Muslims, and the Swahili, and for his general disdain for everything African. And he would express these sentiments with the typical unguarded arrogance of his British colonial mentors. It was for this reason that he came to be popularly known as *Sir* Charles: The Kenyan people were knighting him for his uncompromising support for everything and anything British!

Njonjo's statements were by no means empty verbiage. As indicated above, he was a very influential politician and was extremely adept at manipulating politicians and political situations. His manipulative role in preparing the ground for a coup attempt in 1982 is now public knowledge in Kenya. Again, as indicated above, Njonjo was also the attorney general, the chief law officer of the state. The combination of his political clout and his position as the supreme legal representative of the country, in light of *the corporatist nature of the neocolonial state*, almost gave his utterances in parliament the force of unwritten law.

Indeed, Njonjo's powers were so great that only the extreme autocrat of the country, the late president Jomo Kenyatta, could challenge him. Overruling Njonjo and his supporters, Kenyatta eventually came out in July 1974 to declare Swahili as the national language, and the only language of parliament. But no sooner had Jomo Kenyatta passed away, then Njonjo was able to manipulate the situation to reintroduce English into the Kenyan parliament. The colonial sentiments that were transmitted by Njonjo over twenty years ago have continued to be held by members of some bourgeois and some not-so-bourgeois sections of the east African population. Njonjo's line of opposition to the Swahili was thus successful in casting a grand shadow of doubt not only on the identity of the Swahili people, but also, at least in Kenya, on their very security as citizens and nationals. If, by virtue of the sociolinguistic comparison between Swahili and the English language, the Swahili people had been put at the same level as British colonialist settlers in terms of their citizenship status. What guarantees did they have, in light of other discriminatory evidence, that they would not be targets, sooner or later, of total expropriation and disenfranchisement?

The other level of language attitudes has to do with how a language triggers certain stereotypes about its speaker(s) in the mind of the audience. A classical example of this tendency with regard to the Swahili is described by Jaramogi Oginga Odinga, the first vice-president of Kenya, in his famous book *Not Yet Uhuru*. In particular, Odinga refers to some African adjuncts of the British colonial administration who used to "invade" Luoland periodically to collect taxes. Precisely because these people were themselves not Luo and had no proficiency in the Luo language, they were forced to use a transethnic language of the common Kenyan. To the Luo this created the impression that the tax collectors were Swahili even though there is no record that the Swahili ever participated in collecting taxes in Luoland or elsewhere in Kenya. As a result of this association of the language with the ethnicity of the tax collectors, however, Odinga tells us that the Luo referred to the "Swahili" people as *okoche* (1967:2), a Luo word meaning "vagabond, rogue and cheat." As far westwards as Uganda, in fact, the Swahili language conjures up images of the *bayaye*, the lumpenproletariat, the underclass.

But more important than the negative stereotypes that a language may evoke are the kinds of associations that people sometimes make. A 1981 empirical study by Henry Simiyu demonstrated, using what is called the matched-guise technique[17] in social psychology, that at least Kimvita, the dialect of the Swahili people spoken in Mombasa, Kenya, is overwhelmingly associated with Arab ethnicity and Islam among non-Swahili Africans in Nairobi, the capital of Kenya. On the other hand, standard Swahili prompted non-Swahili African and non-Islamic (mainly Christian) associations. While this study clearly demonstrates that Arabness and Islamness continue to confound Swahili identity, members of the outer-group are conscious of a distinction between the Swahili of the Swahili people — even if they choose to call them Arabs — and the Swahili of the non-Swahili Africans. Even from the perceptions of the outer-groups, therefore, the linguistic definition of Swahili ethnicity in terms of what we have called the "primary" dialects of Swahili still seems justifiable. It indicates a certain degree of acceptance by the average Kenyan, at least, of the Swahili people's own terms of linguistic definition of their identity — even if state functionaries may refuse to acknowledge this state of affairs.

In an empirical language attitude study similar to that of Simiyu, Alamin Mazrui (1981), also utilizing the matched-guise technique, demonstrates the reverse situation. Simiyu's experimental subjects were all non-Swahili; Mazrui's experimental population, on the other hand, was entirely Swahili, though exclusively those of Mombasa. In complete conformity with the findings of Simiyu, Mazrui's study was able to show that standard Swahili was indeed associated with Africans of non-Swahili, and to a lesser extent, of non-Islamic background. Kimvita, on the other hand, was seen as predominantly Swahili/Arab and, to a lesser extent, Islamic in demographic terms. In addition, several specific features of standard Swahili were found unacceptable to the study of population of the Swahili. We may add that while Mazrui's study was based in Kenya, similar sentiments seem to exist among the Swahili of Tanzania.

In both Kenya and Tanzania, in fact, Swahili views towards standard Swahili echo the sentiments of Sheikh Al-Amin Ali Mazrui and Shihabuddin Chiraghdin quoted earlier. Some of the major issues in this connection have been expressed in the following terms by a distinguished Tanzanian Swahili scholar, Sheikh Mohamed Ali, who is also an active member of the Tanzania Swahili Council (BAKITA):

> ... Because our Swahili was not acquired through schooling, it was just received from our parents, we find problems in the area of its usage. Specifically, those of us who speak it as a first language are scorned at, and those who have acquired it through schooling are believed to know better merely because they know how to analyze it. People like me just know how to speak it. But they forget that language is not determined by grammatical rules; it is grammatical rules that are determined by language. People are found to speak in a certain way, which can then be described by grammatical rules. But what we observe these days is that Swahili is being forced to follow grammatical rules and this should not be the case. Now if we agree that grammatical rules should be determined by language, and we are the native speakers of Swahili, reason dictates that we should be consulted. But, instead, we are marginalized very much. There are those who are aware of our stand and they see it

as reasonable. But there are many others who do not appreciate our concerns, especially the schooled to whom Swahili is not their mother tongue. These people started to use Swahili, perhaps, at age six or seven while communicating with other people, or in schools and elsewhere. It is in such places that they make their first acquaintance with Swahili. These are the fortunate ones who had the opportunity to study Swahili and the ones who look down upon those to whom Swahili is their native language. There are some among them who are aware of this dilemma. The Swahili themselves who have learned the structure of their language are indeed very few and they are an uninfluential minority. On the other hand the influence of those to whom Swahili is their second language is tremendous, and these have tried to suppress the opinions of the native speakers of Swahili.

What we are trying to emphasize is that it would be better for the non-Swahili expert of the language to work closely with the native Swahili, to find out how particular concepts and constructions are expressed in the language. Then he should formulate his rules accordingly. But such an idea is not encouraged. It has become a great struggle. Even in places such as the University of Dar es Salaam and in the government where the Swahili language is the focus, a native speaker of Swahili who knows much about his language meets with much resistance, discouragement and sabotage, and is often removed from position because they fear that he may be instrumental in bringing in proper Swahili of "standard" Swahili. Indeed, it is good to have one language which all may understand, because many of the Swahili dialects have many differences. There are many dialectal expressions which are found in one place and not in others. We must, therefore, have a language that works as a standard. It is important that we should have such a language. But we must not allow such a language to be a weapon in obliterating the inherited Swahili.

Those who came with "standard" Swahili have already killed some of the speech sounds. Such people as Frederick Johnson have indeed helped us a great deal to codify the language. But their input has some deficiencies. Some of these deficiencies are found in pronunciation. Instead of "kibiriti" they say "kiberiti," "thamanini," they say "themanini," "kurakibisha," they write "kurekibisha". . . .

Because the Europeans themselves cannot pronounce such words properly, they have forced us to write as they pronounce them. Such distortions have been taught in schools for so long that we as native speakers are now asked to conform to the distorted pronunciations of the foreign Europeans.

My own writings were refused publication because I did not conform to the distorted spellings and pronunciations of "standard" Swahili.... This is the state of Swahili today. But the future looks bright. Both the Swahili themselves and the non-Swahili take much interest and care in its study. I am sure Swahili will advance and I see its advancement as positive.[18]

These sentiments of Sheikh Mohamed Ali of Tanzania, and the views of Sheikh Al-Amin Ali Mazrui and Shihabuddin Chiraghdin quoted earlier, complement the empirical studies of Simiyu and Mazrui to demonstrate that both Swahili and non-Swahili Africans seem to be conscious, even if loosely so, of some linguistic boundary of Swahili ethnicity. And if Mazrui's study manifests some degree of ethnic chauvinism — a phenomenon that is by no means peculiar to the Swahili — and linguistic puritanism, Simiyu's study shows how widely Njonjo's sentiments that associate Swahili with Arabness and Islam have spread in Kenya. This naturally intensifies Swahili fears of expropriation, disenfranchisement, and exclusion from the national politico-economic mainstream. Indeed, it is precisely these kinds of popular sentiments that, in times of increasing economic insecurities, could easily feed autocratic demagoguery targeted against a particular people. The result could be mass expropriation and expulsion as happened to people of Asian origin in Idi Amin's Uganda in the early 1970s.

If the Swahili, therefore, seem to be reacting to the negative views and stereotypes about their language, and if they react towards the changes seemingly being injected into their language, if they seem wary of the attempts to alter the linguistic boundaries of their ethnicity without their explicit participation and consent, it is not because they seek to be unduly purist about their language and ethnicity. It is rather because in the context of east Africa's ethnic politics, their language has become one of the most important symbols of their struggle against expropriation, their struggle for demarginalization, in short their struggle for collective self-preservation. There is little doubt that under different circumstances the "traditional" liberalism that allowed anyone who adopted any variety of Swahili as a first language to be accepted as ethnically Swahili, would have continued without qualification. It is with this in mind, then, that Chiraghdin appealed:

> Tusiche kusema kuwa Kiswahili kina wenyewe, kwani uzuri wake ni kuwa kila akitakaye ni chake. Maana Kiswahili na lugha nyingine za kihuku ni kama "wana wa shangazi na mjomba"; ni ndugu. Basi ikiwa sisi Waafrika tumeweza kujifunza Kiarabu, Kifaransa na Kiingereza mpaka lugha hizo zikakaribia kuwa zetu, kefu Kiswahili kwa Waafrika wa janibu hizi — na hata nyenginezo; wakiki-ingilia hakina budi kuwa kama chao walichozaliwa nacho. Lakini tusijaribu kukikoboa katika mazingira yake halisi. . . . (1973: xi)

> We should not be afraid to say that the Swahili language belongs to a particular people, because there is the positive aspect that whoever wants it can make it his own. Swahili and other languages of this region are like cousins; they are siblings. So, if we as Africans have been able to acquire Arabic, French and English to a point where they have virtually become our languages, how much more Swahili to Africans of this region — and even of other regions; if they go into it, it is bound to be theirs as a native tongue. But we should not attempt to dislodge it from its natural environment. . . .

PART TWO
LITERATURE AND SWAHILI IDENTITY

CHAPTER THREE:
LITERARY HISTORY AND SWAHILI IDENTITY

 has often been assumed that there is an inseparable link between the development of a people's language and their literature. But if that link cannot be broken it can at least be weakened or rendered very fuzzy. The prevailing debate on the language of African literature is a good demonstration of the fuzziness of this supposedly inalienable relationship between language and literature. It is a debate that poses some important questions about the essence of both European and African literatures. What is English literature? Is it the literature of the English people? Or would it include other literatures written in the English language? And need literature be composed in African languages for it to be African? Or would African authorship and African substance be sufficient to delineate an African literature irrespective of the linguistic medium of composition? This line of inquiry, of course, raises a host of other questions: Who is an African? Is there an African literary substance? Would the literature written by South African Boers in Afrikaans be regarded as African?

Similar questions and concerns have now bedeviled the world of "Swahili literature." When the demographic bound-

aries of the Swahili language were coterminous with the boundaries of Swahili ethnicity, literature composed in the Swahili
language could easily have been defined as literature of the
Swahili people. But as in the case of the English, French,
Portuguese, or Spanish, the development and spread of the
Swahili language well beyond its ethnic "borders" has raised
serious questions about the essence of Swahili literature and its
connection with Swahili identity. Topan depicts this scenario
well when he asks:

> Is Swahili literature that literature written only by the
> Waswahili? If so, who is a Mswahili? — itself a controver-
> sial question. Is Swahili literature that literature that deals
> with the Swahili or the East African way of life? Or is
> Swahili literature written by East Africans? (1968:161)

If the public opinion is that there is no Swahili ethnicity, that
there are no people who are cohesive enough as a group to constitute a Swahili ethnic entity, then Swahili literature could easily be defined in unambiguous linguistic terms. It could be any
literature written in the Swahili language. Alternatively, we
could choose to be nationalistic about the issue and define
Swahili literature as that literature which is composed in the
Swahili language and by people whose *national* language is
Swahili.[19] This, then, would include Swahili (language) literature composed by Tanzanians, Kenyans, and, to a lesser extent,
Ugandans. But it would exclude literature in Swahili written by
Europeans, for example. Rainer Arnold is one of the scholars
who, to some extent, takes this view of Swahili literature. In his
opinion, Swahili literature, nowadays,

> . . . represents no more the Swahili culture and society of
> the coast only. But it is part and parcel of the society and cul-
> ture of the new nations of East Africa. From the scientific
> point of view it would certainly be more effective to label
> this literature as East African literature in the Swahili lan-
> guage. . . . (1972-73:69)

The organic development of Swahili literature from a Swahili
ethnic base, therefore, is seen to have been compromised by
forces of linguistic development and political "modernization."

It is possible, of course, to reject the existence of Swahili ethnicity without rejecting the idea of a Swahili identity. As we have indicated before, in Tanzania Swahili has been raised to the level of national identity, and a sense of a Swahili political culture has emerged. Literature composed in the Swahili language by people belonging to this political culture, then, would appropriately be termed Swahili literature. It is this notion of a Swahili political culture that seems to have informed the position taken by Kiango and Sengo when they wrote:

> Kwa hapa kwetu, Kiswahili ndiye mlezi, ametukuza tangu siku za ukoloni na kutuunga pamoja hadi kufika siku za uhuru wetu. Ni lugha inayoeleza utaratibu wetu wa maisha. . . . Mswahili ni Mtanzania na hapana shaka lugha ya Kiswahili ni lugha ya Watanzania. Hivyo, inatazamiwa kwamba watu watakubali kuitwa Waswahili na kujaribu kujenga utamaduni, mila na desturi badala ya kuthamini zaidi ukabila. Na hapa ndipo tutaweza kusema kwamba tunayo fasihi ya Kiswahili. (1972:10)

> Here at home, Swahili is our guardian; it has reared us from the colonial era and united us to the period of our independence. It is the language that expresses our social dynamics. . . . A Swahili means a Tanzanian and there is no doubt that Swahili is the language of Tanzania. Therefore, it is anticipated that people will accept being called Swahili and try to build values, customs and norms instead of placing greater value on ethnicity. And that is when we can say that we have Swahili literature.

The politicization of Swahili identity and its equation with the colonial creation called the nation-state is, of course, a phenomenon that is primarily Tanzanian. Even though Swahili is also the national language of Kenya, the idea that a Kenyan is also a Swahili would be alien indeed to the people of that country, at least for the foreseeable future. But this is not the case in Tanzania, where ethnicities are seen as getting increasingly subsumed under a national ethos with Swahili as its binding force. It is in this connection that Lodhi, essentially supporting Kiango and Sengo, comments:

The Tanzanian culture, therefore, is the sum total of all the good customs and traditions of the different language groups in Tanzania. All these regional cultures using local languages, or dialects, are now being transformed into a National Culture using Swahili which is increasingly commanding the loyalty, affection and respect of Tanzanians. (1974:11)

But if Swahili literature is defined in these terms it would automatically exclude the literature in Swahili composed by the Swahili as well as non-Swahili people of non-Tanzanian origin. This is definitely a difficult proposition to accept.

Senkoro, on the other hand, still inspired by the Tanzanian concept of Swahili identity, proposes a definition that goes beyond the nation-state:

Mwanzoni tulitaja uhusiano wa fasihi na utamaduni wa jamii inayohusika. Uhusiano huu utatusaidia hapa katika kueleza ushairi wa Kiswahili. Tutaamua kuwa kazi fulani ni ya fasihi ya Kiswahili au la kutokana na jinsi ilivyojitambulisha na ilivyojihusisha na utamaduni wa Kiswahili. Hapa neno Waswahili halimaanishi kabila la Waswahili kwani kabila la namna hiyo halipo leo. Waswahili hapa ni wananchi wa Afrika ya masharika na kati kwa jumla na wala si wale tu wanaoishi katika pwani ya nchi hizi. (1988:11)

At the beginning we talked about the relationship between literature and culture of the related society. This relationship will help us in defining Swahili poetry. We shall decide that a particular work is or is not Swahili literature on the basis of its projection of and relationship with the culture of the Swahili people. Here the term Swahili does not mean an ethnic group of the Swahili people, for such an ethnic group does not exist today. The Swahili people here are citizens of East and Central Africa in general and not only those who live on the coastline of these countries.

Senkoro thus posits a transnational Swahili culture whose literature, if it is written in the Swahili language and deals with and reflects that culture, would appropriately be defined as Swahili literature.

Along more or less the same lines as Senkoro, but without the cultural association, Robert Philipson argues for a supranational Swahili literature that would include literature in the Swahili language, and not necessarily by "Swahili" people or on "Swahili" culture, from Tanzania, Kenya, and Uganda. This supranational literature, according to Philipson, should also take into account the participation and contribution of the Swahili-speaking communities of Zaire (Philipson 1990:20). In fact, one may go further and suggest the concept of *Swahiliphone Africa*, which would include Kenya, Tanzania, Uganda, Comoro Islands, and certain demographic sections of Zaire, Somalia, Sudan, Mozambique, Rwanda, Burundi, and Malawi. Swahili literature, then, would be defined as Swahiliphone literature in the Swahili language.

It seems to us, however, that the positions taken by Kiango and Sengo, and by Arnold and Philipson properly belong to the sphere of *literature in Swahili*. They, at least implicitly, avoid the possibility of a Swahili literature as an ethnic literature of the Swahili people. The implication here, then, is that what is called Swahili literature can no longer be used as an attribute of Swahili ethnic identity. The Swahili people, in other words, can no longer claim to have a literature in the Swahili language that is distinctly theirs and that can promote their collective consciousness and identity.

The problem with these conceptions, however, is that they view Swahili literature in terms of a frozen moment that stretches from the inception of European colonial rule to the present. This literature is heterogenous ethnically, nationally, religiously, as well as ideologically. It is transethnic and transnational literature whose only binding force is a Swahili language that, although differentiated, tends to revolve around the standard norm. Swahili as well as non-Swahili, Tanzanian as well as non-Tanzanian, Muslim as well as non-Muslim authors have all participated in, and contributed to, the creation of this literature. This literature is also both oral and written, but when written it tends to be based on the Latin script.

But Swahili literature does not begin with the inception of European colonial rule. In fact, there is no reason to assume that the Swahili people did not become aware of the written word at an early phase in their development and contact with the Arab world. This does not mean, however, that writing was immediately adopted in the composition of their literature. In its formation the literature of this emergent Swahili people may have remained exclusively oral for centuries. And when writing was introduced it may have initially been restricted to recording oral compositions. Composing in the written medium, therefore, may have been one of the later functions for which writing was used once introduced into Swahili society.

Having said all this, however, we must hasten to add that the history of creative writing among the Swahili cannot be taken to have begun with the availability of the earliest known document. This kind of deductive reasoning implies that only that which can be documented can be presumed to have existed. It is this kind of textual attitude towards real history that may have led to the most prolific scholar on Swahili literature to regard A.D. 1728 as the point of inception of Swahili literature (by which we suppose the writer means written literature) [Knappert, 1971:5]. As it turns out, the University of Dar-es Salaam has in its collection a Swahili literary document that dates as early as the fourteenth century, and there is no good reason to presume that Swahili creative writing using the Arabic script could not have started long before the fourteenth century. We need to be particularly wary of the pitfalls of this "documentarist ideology," especially in connection with a society that, at least until recently, placed a different kind of value on the written word from the societies of the northern hemisphere. As a result of this value difference, the Swahili were less zealous about preserving their documented literature than many northern scholars would like to assume. And the outcome may have been the loss of a wealth of preexisting written literature. This is not to mention the fact that manuscripts that were preserved tended to deteriorate rapidly under the impact of the tropical climate.

At the present stage of our knowledge, it is not possible to determine the point in time when Swahili's oral literature — the *ngano*, the *nyimbo*, the *misemo*, the *vitendawili*, etc.— came to be complemented with a written literature initially based, of course, on the Arabic script. We do know, however, that creative writing in Swahili in this script was overwhelmingly biased towards poetry, and that "religious" poetry always had a better chance of being preserved in the written form than did composition of more profane kinds. Until a few decades ago, Swahili prose remained essentially oral. Some of these narratives had local origins, both Swahili and non-Swahili (e.g., Somali, Boni, Pokomo, Mijikenda, and Zaramo), while some others were local adaptations of otherwise nonlocal (especially Arabian and Persian) extraction. In addition to its local allegoric tales and animal fables, myths, and legends, the Swahili oral literary tradition came to be enriched with localized prose from Arab-Persian sources. In addition, narratives with Islamic themes, especially those revolving around the lives of prophets and apostles, came to be featured quite significantly in the Swahili oral prose tradition. The function of much of this oral dimension of Swahili literature was, of course, didactic.

In the meantime, however, a whole tradition of composing poetry and preserving it in a written medium using the Arabic script developed among the Swahili. Much of this poetry tended to be homiletic. As in the case of the Hausa-Fulani, poetry came to serve as an important means of spiritual engagement among the Swahili. Until well into the British colonial period, for example, it was not uncommon to find a poem like *Al-Inkishafi* being recited in mosques and Islamic *madrasahs*. In a sense, Swahili homiletic verse became part of a whole corpus of Islamic materials belonging to a literacy-based instructional tradition.

In any case, such was the state of affairs that the Germans and the British encountered when they set foot on the east coast of Africa: there was a strong, flourishing, multidimensional oral tradition, combining prose and poetry, and a written literary mode that was heavily biased towards homiletic verse. This literature coincided directly with a distinct ethnicity, a literature produced by the Swahili themselves, using their respective Swahili regional dialects, and concentrating on themes that were directly or indirectly tied to their socio-cultural milieu.

The inception of British colonial rule brought with it its own impact on Swahili literature. The Arabic script that had hitherto been used in Swahili literature was, of course, largely confined to east Africa's Muslim population. It was a script acquired in the process of Qur'anic and Islamic education. The British now introduced the Latin script and through the school and church, made it accessible to a wide trans-Swahili population of east Africans. Literacy in the Latin script would now expose non-Swahili people to the world of Swahili literature, eventually leading to the emergence of non-Swahili literary composers in the Swahili language. The British colonial influence also prompted the extension of the Swahili *ngano* (story) to the novel, the Swahili *tungo/mashairi ya kujibizana* (dramatized performances of dialogue poetry) perhaps to the play, and the Swahili *tungo/mashairi* to free verse. Having so grown, Swahili language literature became increasingly trans-Swahili in terms of the ethnic background of its authors, the nature of its themes, the multiplicity of its genres, as well as its Swahili dialects of composition. The ethnic "de-Swahilization" of Swahili literature had thus become a reality.

But, precisely because of the ethnic differences in eastern Africa's literary histories and traditions, it would be rather unrealistic to assume that the nature and magnitude of the European impact on Swahili literature was the same throughout the region. The colonial experience did introduce new genres and subgenres in the world of literature composed in the Swahili language. But the development of these forms among ethnically Swahili writers was bound to be linked to their pre-twentieth century literary tradition. The colonial encounter, in other words, served as an impetus for a fresh organic progression of the literature of the Swahili people. The novels of modern writers like Mohamed S. Mohamed and Said Mohamed have a certain affinity with the novels of Euphrase Kezilahabi and F.E.M.K. Senkoro, both non-Swahili in ethnic terms. But the novels also betray stylistic differences that are clearly ethnically derived. The modern (i.e., post-nineteenth century) writings of the Swahili people, then, belong to their expanding ethnic tradition as well as to the wider, transethnic regional experience. It is at once ethnic and, paradoxically, transethnic.

Against this backdrop, then, in addition to a linguistic definition, *Swahili literature* can also be defined ethnically as that literature composed in the Swahili language by the Swahili people. This literature would include in its ambit the precolonial literature composed in the Swahili language. Its Swahili dialects may be standard or akin to it or drawn from the primary dialects. It is also both oral and written, but the written

word may be in Arabic or Latin script. Its themes may be cul-
ture-bound to Swahili ethnicity or based on non-Swahili or even
trans-Swahili experiences. It is a literature that has certain historical continuities that stretch from very old times to the present. And it is this historicity we believe that is at the root of the
literary consciousness of the Swahili people, adding a literary
dimension to their sense of collective identity.

There is no doubt, however, that precisely because precolonial Swahili literature was more clearly coincident with their
own particular ethnicity, it has come to assume a special place
in the ethnic consciousness of the Swahili people. Yet, in the
study of Swahili literature, it is precisely this pre-twentieth century tradition of Swahili literature that has been subjected most
to misrepresentations, some of which deform the very essence
of Swahili identity. Some of these misrepresentations have
resulted from the Arab-Islamic bias and others from the modal
bias of Eurocentric scholarship. It is to a discussion of these
misrepresentations that we will now turn.

The Arab-Islamic bias prevailing in discussions of the Swahili
people and the Swahili language also found its way into the
study of Swahili literature. The following excerpts from the
writings of Jan Knappert are not atypical of the views that pre-
vail in the general run of academic scholarship as regards the
historical substance of pre-twentieth century Swahili literature
in its entirety:

> To trace the origin of each aspect of Swahili culture, liter-
> ature and mythology back to its roots in one of the Oriental
> lands will require another volume and several more years
> of intensive study. In some cases I have been able to discover
> the origin of a Swahili legend in Arabic or Sanskrit literature.
> (1967: 7-8)

> Swahili literature is profoundly immersed in its [Islamic]
> spirit. The Koran, the legends of the Prophet Muhammad
> and the other prophets and Saints of Islam, points of doc-
> trine and theology are referred to on every page of tradi-
> tional Swahili literature. (1979: XIX)

> Swahili literature, both prose and poetry, is full of refer-
> ences to Islamic law, and of admonitions to the faithful to

observe it in every detail. A knowledge of Islamic law is essential for understanding Swahili literature, especially with regard to marriage and family law. (1979: XVIII)

A quick survey of Swahili poetry at every stage in its history reveals how mistaken Knappert's opinions are. About no point of their history can one say that the Swahili produced a greater proportion of homiletic verse than secular verse. This Orientalist bias in the study of the so-called traditional Swahili literature becomes even more apparent when we compare Swahili poetic collections in the Swahili language with those in English. The Swahili collections would include : *Diwani ya Muyaka bin Haji al-Ghassany* (Hichens, 1940), *Masomo Yenye Adili* (Robert, 1959), *Sheria za Kutunga Mashairi na Diwani ya Amri* (Adedi, 1954), *Malenga wa Mvita* (Bhalo, 1971), *Sauti ya Dhiki* (Abdalla, 1975), *Malenga wa Mrima* (Mohamed, 1977), *'Sikate Tamaa* (Mohamed, 1981), among others. All these collections deal with verse that, thematically, is essentially secular.[20] On the other hand we have several books on Swahili poetry written in English by European scholars. Noteworthy among these are *Swahili Poetry* (Harries, 1962), *Traditional Swahili Poetry* (Knappert, 1967), three volumes of *Swahili Islamic Poetry* (Knappert, 1971), and *Tendi* (Allen, 1971). These collections tend to concentrate on poetic themes that are essentially religious. This divergence in focus between Swahili collections and English collections of Swahili poetry in what we may call the "traditional" mode, we contend, is not accidental. Rather, it is rooted, again, in two other biases of the Eurocentric paradigm: a "modal" and a "racial" bias.

The modal bias concerns the values imposed upon the written word. The written, even if peripheral, is thus given prominence over the oral, even if the latter is more central in a given tradition. As intimated above, before the Swahili people themselves began producing collections of their poetry in the Latin script, much of the so-called traditional Swahili verse that was secular existed essentially in the oral mode, while it was homiletic verse that tended to be recorded or composed in the written mode using the Arabic script, thanks largely to the outlooks and preferences of the social strata that were the most directly engaged in preparing and preserving written documents. It is this written literature, therefore, that came to define virtually the entire scope of Swahili literature in Eurocentric scholarship, which has operated in Africa on a quasi-Cartesian philosophy: "I write, therefore I am," while the unwritten is presumed to be nonexistent as well.

The racial bias, on the other hand, is the one that operates on the Germanic hierarchy of "races": European > Oriental > African. If the Oriental "race" is somewhat superior to the African, then what is Oriental naturally becomes more preeminent and, therefore, more deserving of intellectual focus than that which is African. Hence the "African" in Swahili literature is submerged by the undue focus on its "Orientality." The modal and racial biases are of course not unrelated. The British colonialists, for example, generally tended to regard more highly those societies with a written tradition than those with an oral tradition alone. The "modal" and "racial" biases of Eurocentricity thus combined on the shores of Swahililand to "conspire" against Swahili literature's secular verse in favor of its Islamic verse that supposedly betrays its Oriental connections.

There are European scholars, however, who acknowledge that, at least in the last century before British colonialism, traditional Swahili literature was not entirely homiletic. Commenting on the poetry that appeared in the local press in Tanganyika, for example, Lyndon Harries wrote :

> This wider modern practice of Swahili versification has led to a departure from its earlier intention to express the spirit and practice of Islam. Today the mechanism is employed for more secular ends. Any news item may be the subject of a few verses, but this is the tradition established during the nineteenth century by writers like Muyaka bin Haji of Mombasa, who brought poetry out of the mosque and into the market-place. (Harries, 1962:2)

In other words Muyaka (ca. 1776-1856) is regarded as the historical turning point of Swahili poetry: Swahili secular verse is presumed to have emerged during the "Muyaka era."

This conclusion by Harries is yet again a product of the modal bias of Eurocentricity. For it is not at all clear how Harries could have drawn the conclusion that Muyaka was the first Swahili poet to compose secular verse. This view has probably been influenced by the production in print, in the *written* word, of Hichens' collection of Muyaka's poetry.[21] It was as if the appearance in *print* of Muyaka's verse led to a sudden awakening that Swahili does indeed have a verse that is not religious. It is possible that had it not been for the publication of this anthology, secular verse in Swahili literature might have come to be regarded as an exclusively twentieth century affair. Thus, the modal bias in Eurocentric scholarship has influenced views not only on the longevity of Swahili secular verse, but also on the longevity of the entire verse tradition of the Swahili people. This relates to the saga of Fumo Liyongo. Apart from being the earliest known hero in Swahili folklore, Liyongo is also regarded by the Swahili people as the earliest Swahili poet of note whose works are believed to have survived to this day. Just as the person of Muyaka has become central to the question of the longevity of Swahili secular verse, Liyongo has come to personify the debate on the longevity of Swahili poetry in general. But to the Swahili people, of course, Liyongo has meant more than this. As one of the authors of this text has previously written, Liyongo became

> an almost iconic representation of the depth, the achievement and the ambience of the culture as a whole. That he lived a thousand years ago, more or less, has come to symbolize the longevity of the poetic tradition as well as the early achievement of excellence within this tradition. That Fumo Liyongo was at once a major poet and a "hero" in the social world makes him, for the collective imagination, the embodiment of that combination of the poetic utterance and social practice which epitomizes the Swahili ideal of a fully developed human potential. (Shariff, 1991:153-4)

The figure of Fumo Liyongo, then, is deeply embedded in the literary and cultural imagination of the Swahili people, and dating Liyongo becomes intimately tied to the historical consciousness and identity of this group.

The modal bias of Eurocentric scholarship, however, has questioned the depth of this historical tradition, restricting its tenure to a period for which documentary evidence is available. For example, Knappert states:

> It is probably safe to establish the date of Liyongo's death as 1690 or earlier. How much earlier will always remain a reason for controversy. Professor Freeman-Grenville places Liyongo about 1580. James Kirkman, too, believes that he may have lived around AD 1600. (1979:66)

This contrasts sharply with the position of scholars who have relied more heavily on the oral tradition. These include Chiraghdin (1973:1), Hichens (1939:51), and Harries (1962:6), who have tended to place Liyongo's existence sometime between the ninth and thirteenth centuries. In essence then, the difference of opinion centers on whether Liyongo existed earlier (i.e., during the pre-Portuguese period) or later, (i.e., during the Portuguese period) in east Africa.

The issue of Liyongo's period of existence, however, has implications not only for the longevity of the Swahili literary tradition, but also for the religious constitution of their faith. The Swahili people are predominantly Muslim, and in their oral accounts they have all along regarded Liyongo as sharing not only in their art and culture but also in their faith. Islam has been such a central accompanying feature of Swahili identity that to claim that Liyongo was not a Muslim is to border on the claim that he was not a Swahili. Such a claim, in other words, would undermine not only the history of the Swahili culture but also the historical consciousness of the Swahili people. If Liyongo lived sometime between the ninth and thirteen centuries, and if by then Islam had already become a feature of Swahili identity (Horton, 1987:88), it is inconceivable to the Swahili mind that their poet-hero, Fumo Liyongo, was anything but a Muslim. By historically placing him in the era of the Portuguese, however, Knappert created room for speculation that Liyongo may have been a Christian (1979:68; see also 92) and not, as previously believed, a Muslim.

In a recent article, however, one of the authors (Shariff, 1991) was able to demonstrate that the Swahili oral account is supported by archeological evidence presented by Mark Horton (1987) in placing Fumo Liyongo prior to the fourteenth century, long before the inception of the Portuguese period in east Africa. In the same article Shariff also showed that while the attempted "Christianization" of Fumo Liyongo rests on a misreading of certain aspects of Swahili history and poetry, it has sometimes been based on deliberate distortions and manipulation of literary information.

To recapitulate, then, the period of Liyongo's existence has long been a matter of conjecture among scholars trained in Eurocentric paradigms. To a large extent, the quest for Liyongo's dates seems to have been based on an innocent scholarly pursuit despite the fact that it has tended to put Swahili literary history in doubt. There are a few scholars, however, who seem to have capitalized on this area of conjecture to attribute to Liyongo a religious faith other than the one popularly associated with Swahili identity — Islam. A careful look at the line of reasoning that affiliates Liyongo with the Christian faith reveals, we believe, a scholarly motive that is less than innocent. The attempt belongs to a chain of Eurocentric arguments seemingly intended to throw Swahili identity even further into a conceptual disarray.

Literary misrepresentations, however, may result not only from the historical mislocation of compositions, but also from the misinterpretation of their content. Since the inception of European colonial rule in east Africa, Swahili literature has undergone an expansion not only in terms of form, number of genres, and variety of themes, but also in terms of the functions to which literature is put. European education "elevated" the schooled African, cordoned him off from the rest of his society, and assigned to him an abstract, intellectual-reflective function for his literary creativity that was hitherto unknown in the Swahili community. Prior to that the composition of Swahili poetry was predominantly bound by social context and social events. The fit between poetry and the rest of society was in fact so tight that poetic language was often an expressive mode of regular, social communication. Through its total merger with society, poetic language thus became the ideal marker of conversational elegance in normal social interaction.

The pervasive social contextuality of Swahili poetry mandates that the precise and full semantic scope of a particular poem cannot be discovered without some knowledge of the social cir-

cumstances of its composition. To this day it is not uncommon
to find two or more Swahili interlocutors arguing about the
particular person or the particular event to which a song playing on the radio may precisely be referring. It is a literary tradition that is so deeply ingrained in the consciousness of the
average Swahili person that the idea of a poem composed in the
abstract without reference to a particular social being, social
events, or a social context, is unlikely to cross his mind. In one
of his books, Harries comments:

> . . . it is essential first to emphasize the difficulty any
> Westerner must have in estimating the worth of poetry writ-
> ten in a foreign language often concerning local situations
> and happenings. It would be wrong to attempt an assess-
> ment only from a study of the texts as provided in this book.
> Many of the poems were meant to be sung and intoned and
> have a social and religious value which the bare texts may
> not reveal. Poems of the nineteenth century were often writ-
> ten to suit an immediate historical situation. It may be that
> even after the most diligent investigation we cannot recap-
> ture the exact implication of a verse because we may not be
> able to reconstruct the exact situation. There are hundreds
> of short Swahili poems in the library of the School of
> Oriental and African Studies in London which still defy
> interpretation partly because no one is able to provide the
> context in which the poem was written. (Harries, 1962:2)

This is a comment that would come as no surprise to a Swahili
person who, as a matter of artistic habit, is accustomed to associating poems with social contexts.

But precisely because of its contextuality, pre-twentieth century Swahili poetry has been vulnerable to easy misinterpretation. Poems have been preserved whose social contexts are
unknown and their interpretation has been left to the genius,
resourcefulness, and creativity of individual scholars. A scholar
may choose to be rigorous, thorough, and honest in seeking the
context of a particular poem, thereby reaching an interpretation
that is more or less correct and probably in conformity with the
sensibilities of the Swahili people. Or he may choose to use the
"inaccessibility" of context to arrive at an interpretation that
suits his particular ideological interests. A scholar may also be

an innocent victim of misinformation, leading to interpretations that are wrong, though well-intentioned. Once written, such interpretations become subject to the modal bias of Eurocentric scholarship regardless of the motivations of particular scholars. They get propagated by those trained in Eurocentric scholarship who have come to regard the printed word as something sacred. In this way well-intentioned but erroneous interpretations of a people are reinforced and ultimately associated with their identity.

When one reads Knappert's (1979) interpretations of many Swahili poems, for example, one is likely to be left with the impression that the Swahili have serious sexual and romantic fixations. Knappert has, perhaps inadvertently, led us to a paradox: the poetry that is said to be deeply immersed in the Islamic spirit is at the same time erotic and sensual. Sexual interpretations are presented as matter of fact, without any effort on the part of the author to provide the social context of the poems analyzed. When a social context is provided, it is often a product of the author's own imagination. In his 1979 publication, Knappert thus reaches some false and bizarre conclusions that, for example, in Swahili society, "[t]he food on which a fly has settled," symbolizes "a girl who is no longer a virgin" (52), "a cat is a frequent symbol for a lover" or "lady-killer" (56), and "[c]oconut juice is a symbol of virginity, of feminine beauty" (56).

The danger of depicting a people in certain images is by no means limited to the interpretation of poetic content. It could equally well apply to the selection of examples to make a particular point. For instance, in discussing the themes of the Swahili *nyimbo* (songs), Ohly writes:

> Among the works that have been preserved, social contradictions often appear: for instance a slave-girl and a free girl are regarded as equal by the lover, and yet the slave seen as one of Satan's brood. (1985: 467)

This example essentially reintroduces the pet colonial theme of slavery in Swahili culture. But Ohly does not tell us which song he is referring to: Does it really exist or is it merely a figment of his imagination? When making this statement, was he interested in the real thematic trend in Swahili songs or merely in pandering to those aroused by the exotic? If such a theme does indeed exist in Swahili songs, then, we contend, it is more an exception than a rule. So why would a very widely read scholar, as Ohly definitely is, give the slave theme prominence above more common themes of social contradictions? Indeed, this is like isolating a single bacterium from a bacteria-infested duodenum and magnifying it to a degree that makes other bacteria invisible. Where there has been a whole history of misinformation against a people, such scholarship with its selective magnification of examples can only aggravate the distortion about them and cloud their identity.

In summary, then, we began this chapter by suggesting that while the term *Swahili literature* can be defined linguistically as that literature composed in the Swahili language, it could also be understood in ethnic terms as the literature of the Swahili people. One could say that the impact of European literature on the precolonial literature of the Swahili people produced a synthesis that is uniquely Swahili in ethnic terms. The history and interpretation of the literature of the Swahili composed in the precolonial period, however, have sometimes been subjected to distortions and misrepresentations touching upon the longevity and substance of the Swahili literary tradition. This has tended to confound the literary expression of Swahili identity.

The literary dimension of Swahili identity, however, is "complicated" not only by questions of Swahili literary history and interpretation, but also by considerations of literary form and quality. In the following chapter, then, we shall look at these latter aspects of Swahili literature as they impact on the issue of Swahili identity.

CHAPTER FOUR:
LITERARY FORM
AND SWAHILI IDENTITY

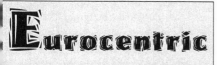 scholarship has sometimes set some dangerous precedents, not only in relation to the study of Swahili literary history and the interpretation of Swahili literary content, but also in determining standards of literary quality. The Swahili and other African peoples have long had their own criteria for judging what is and what is not a good poem, which is the best and which is the worst literary composition. But colonial Eurocentricism came with its own aesthetic paradigms that it imposed on African societies. The result was a derailment of the indigenous African literary traditions. New standards set by outsiders took their place.

The Eurocentric paradigm of literary aesthetics has often portended to be blind to literary content: The beauty of a composition is supposedly judged by its formalistic qualities, its language, its imagery, its symbolism, and so forth. This, however, is not always the case. There have been instances where a literary composition is accorded aesthetic superiority, not because of its style, but because of a content that serves particular ideological ends. James Mbotela's *Uhuru wa Watumwa*, it seems to us, is just one such composition.

In terms of its literary quality, *Uhuru wa Watumwa* is clearly a substandard work, whether we apply Swahili aesthetic criteria or English ones. The language is unengaging and lacking in virtually all the attributes of elegance normally associated with Swahili literary style. There is little artistry by way of characterization: The characters of *Uhuru wa Watumwa* are generally flat, undeveloped, and static. The plot's structure is rather uninteresting, and the text lacks even the basic elements of African oral literature that could give it some rhythm and vibrancy. In short, the value of the book lies only in being one of a pioneering set of Swahili prose texts to be *written* by local people in the Latin script.

Despite its many "literary flaws," which would normally lead a European to regard it as a worthless work of art, C. G. Richards ironically claims that *Uhuru wa Watumwa* "is acknowledged to be one of the best works of Swahili prose produced in this century" (1956:5). But who is it that has acknowledged *Uhuru wa Watumwa* to be one of the best Swahili prose writings of the twentieth century? This is certainly not the view of the Swahili people, nor is it the opinion of east Africans familiar with Swahili literature. We do not know of a single east African literary critic who regards *Uhuru wa Watumwa* as deserving of merit. It is only the British who regard this unartistic work as one of the century's best, and one must question their motives in praising it.

Uhuru wa Watumwa deals with the theme of "Arab slavery" and with British abolition efforts. It posits, on the one hand, Arabs, Swahili, and Muslims as slave-traders and the worst of villains, and on the other hand, Europeans and Christians as selfless saviors and protectors of the victims of the east African slave trade. In describing the intentions, efforts, and concerns of the British, for example, Mbotela writes:

"Uiweke Mungu, ikue dola ya Waingereza."
Ndivyo walivyokuwa wakisema hao wazazi wetu: Kama si Waingereza, hatujui tungekuwa wapi leo! Mwingereza hapendi utumwa. Hao Wazungu mashujaa Dr. Livingstone na wengineo, waliona mambo maovu sana yakitendeka katika bara Afrika: watu weusi wakisumbuliwa kwa kuuzwa huku na huku. Hawakuvumilia kunyamaza, ila walichongea huko kwao Ulaya, ubaya ule uliokuwa ukiendelea katika nchi ya Afrika. Nchi nzima ya Uingereza iliudhika waliposikia taabu ya Waafrika. Dola nzima ya Malkia Victoria, iliingiwa na huruma juu ya watu weusi. Hicho kilio chao kilifanya Waingereza wawe mashujaa katika kuipeleleza Afrika ya ndani. Manowari zao zilitanga

huku na huku kutafuta na kuwaokoa watumwa waliokuwa
katika majahazi ya Waarabu. (31-2)

"Preserve, O God, and extend the reign of the British
Empire."
This is what our parents used to say: Had it not been for
the British, we do not know where we should be today! The
Briton does not like slavery. Those brave Europeans, Dr.
Livingstone and others, witnessed the evil deeds being carried out on the African continent: black people tortured by
being sold hither and thither. They could not bear to remain
silent, but reported to their home in Europe the evil that
was going on in Africa. The whole of Britain was distressed
when they learned about the troubles Africans faced. The
entire dominion of Queen Victoria felt pity for the Africans.
Their lamentation made the British courageous in exploring
the African interior. Their men-of-war patrolled all over
looking for and freeing slaves in Arab dhows.

Clearly, then, the British had "discovered" in *Uhuru wa
Watumwa* an African articulation of a colonial ideology that not
only legitimized their colonial presence but also exonerated
them for all time to come.

While Mbotela's book was targeted mainly against Arabs,
Muslims, and the Swahili, there is no doubt that it quickly came
to be seen as the African text *par excellence* to advocate European
imperialism in Africa. The British slave "saviors" had now
turned the Mbotelas into mental slaves, becoming staunch
advocates of a new kind of European bondage for their African
kith and kin. It is for this reason that one of James Mbotela's
sons "was assassinated in 1953 for his bold stand against those
[Mau Mau] who were attempting to bring a kind of terror to this
land" (Richards, 1956:5).

It is the procolonialist ideological content of *Uhuru wa
Watumwa*, then, that seems to have prompted the British to pro-
claim it as one of the Swahili's best works in the twentieth century. The British did not believe this, of course, but it served as
a good artistic pretext for introducing the book into schools and
having it read widely throughout east Africa. The great dis-
junction between the Swahili *Uhuru wa Watumwa* and its
English translation *The Freeing of the Slaves in East Africa* betrays

efforts at making the book more "readable" in English (in contrast to its Swahili version). Major differences exist in the structure and content between the Swahili and English versions of the book. The English version was obviously "doctored" for an audience that had to be convinced of the literary worth of *Uhuru wa Watumwa*, that was not simply a cheap apology for colonialism. The British were willing to compromise their own standards of literary quality if by so doing their colonial interests were enhanced. The result in this case was a celebrated work of Swahili literature that was anti-Swahili and undermined Swahili identity.

In more recent times, the "problem" of Swahili literary quality has come to feature most prominently in the area of poetry, and more specifically in connection with prosodic form. Like the question of literary history, aspects of literary form may have definite implications for the question of identity. People tend to identify their literature not only in terms of its language and content, but also in terms of the peculiarities of its form. As indicated earlier, pre-twentieth century Swahili literary form precluded the novel, the play, and free verse in its modern manifestations. These are more recent Swahili genres and subgenres, which are a product of the encounter with European colonialism in the twentieth century. How, then, did the Swahili respond to this infusion of new literary forms into their literature?

Interestingly enough, the Swahili have never objected to the emergence of the novel and the play in Swahili literature. These genres seem to have been regarded almost as organic extensions of the preexisting *ngano* (story) and *mashairi ya kujibizana* (dialogic poetry), respectively. But the introduction of free verse[22] was quick to stir the indignation of the Swahili intelligentsia. There are probably two reasons for this development. First, between the *ngano* and the novel, and between dramatic poetry and the play, there has been a difference in the very mode of presentation: oral versus written modes. In a sense then, the novel and the play assumed a life of their own, separate from, even if extensions of, the *ngano* and dramatic poetry. But since Swahili poetry was already written, the introduction of free verse in the written mode was viewed as tampering with the Swahili poetic organism. While both operated within the written mode, free verse was seen to be in competition with "prosodic" verse.[23] Second, writing tends to give its material a certain kind of prominence and immutability. People become much more passionately attached to the character of their written word, because its seeming permanence enhances a sense of their collective identity. A society, therefore, may be less flexible in accommodating changes in its written literature than in its oral literature. The Swahili have been less accommodating to changes in their written poetry than in their *ngano,* which had remained exclusively oral.

Against this backdrop, then, the negative reaction to free verse by the Swahili people was to be expected. This response, however, produced a counterreaction that challenged the very genesis of Swahili prosodic verse, leading to a debate that has polarized Swahili poetry around its African axis, on the one hand, and foreign (Arab/European) axis, on the other. Two central dimensions of this debate have been the prosody and the language of Swahili poetry. And it is to a discussion of these aspects that we shall now turn.

There was a sense in which the introduction of free verse in Swahili poetry was projected as a liberating force from the fetters of prosodic formalism. And breaking away from this Swahili poetic "tradition" was itself regarded as a bold and courageous pioneering act intended to free the Swahili creative impulse. It is probably in reaction to this mood among the proponents of free verse that led Chiraghdin to claim that this mode of composition was prompted less by courage than by a sense of insecurity. The "new" poets had supposedly turned to a "foreign" mode of composition because they felt inadequate to compose in the traditional mold. According to Chiraghdin:

> Waliosema ati watu waliojaribu tungo za kigeni zisizo na fungamano lolote na Arudhi ya Kiswahili ni mashujaa kwa kuwa ati wameikata minyororo na kujitoa pingu za utungaji wa mashairi ya Kiswahili, hawajasema lolote la maana, kwani mtu hutokaje katika pingamizi za fani maalumu ikiwa kamwe fani yenyewe haimweli? . . . Hao wajigambao na hawana la kujigambia, wameambiwa tangu kale:
> Howe! Wapigaje howe! nyama usijamfuma?
> Howe! akali mwituni, na maguuye mazima.

Howe! nda mwenye kufuma, wewe una howe gani?
(1971:13)

Those who say that people who have experimented with
foreign compositions which have no relationship whatso-
ever with Kiswahili prosody are courageous, because they
have supposedly broken the chains and freed themselves
from the fetters of Swahili poetic composition, have not said
anything of substance, for how does one escape the confines
of a particular discipline when that discipline is completely
incomprehensible to him?. . . Those who boast, without having anything to boast for, have long been told:
Hooray! Why shout hooray! When you haven't shot the
prey?
Hooray! It's still in the wild, with its legs intact.
Hooray? That's for the successful hunter; whence comes
your hooray?!

Chiraghdin thus likens the emergent free verse poets to a hunter
who uses an impotent foreign weapon (European free style) to
hunt a sophisticated and elusive animal prey (Swahili prosodic
style); a hunter who boasts and becomes jubilant when, in fact,
he has not accomplished his mission. To Chiraghdin then,
Swahili free verse is a nonstarter, a foreign body in the Swahili
poetic organism that, though composed in Swahili, should be
regarded as non-Swahili in its literary value. This is a sentiment
that is shared by many Swahili cultural nationalists.

Of course, Chiraghdin is wrong on virtually all counts: First,
a number of the proponents of free verse have demonstrated
that they can compose in prosodic style as easily as they can
compose in free style; they have not proved inadequate in operating within the confines of meter and rhyme. Second, while
these "new" poets may indeed find free verse liberating for
them — a development that perhaps deserves a "hooray" —
there is no evidence, prior to the emergence of this debate, that
they sought the demise of Swahili's prosodic tradition.
Chiraghdin's statements, therefore, must be seen to some extent
against the backdrop of the insecurities of Swahili identity. If
there was anything in Swahili identity that had attained cultural
weight of some permanence it was the prosodic tradition, the
oldest Swahili artistic tradition to have existed in written form.

On the other hand, the proponents of free verse seemed predominantly non-Swahili, or Swahili who are "alienated" products of Eurocentric scholarship. What was merely an experiment in Swahili free verse, then, was seen by Swahili nationalists as yet another attempt to redefine the parameters of Swahili identity *from without*. The fear was, and perhaps continues to be, that the terms of Swahili identity were being defined by "interest groups" other than the Swahili. It was an understandable, though unjustifiable, reaction from a people who felt their identity was at stake. It is this consideration perhaps that led Tigiti wa Sengo, in response to the claims of advocates of free verse, to say:

> Ushairi wa Kiswahili kama ulivyo ushairi wa Kingoni, wa Kinyamwezi au wa Kimakonde ni urithi wa utamaduni wa watu wa jamii maalumu. Utaalamu wake utatokana na kukuzwa na utamaduni huo ama kwa kuukubali, kuuthamini na kujifunza kiasi cha kuwa na wewe watunga na kukubalika kuwa una kipawa cha utungaji. (1978:v)

> Swahili poetry, like Ngoni, Nyamwezi or Makonde poetry is the cultural heritage of people of a specific society. Its mastery will derive from growing up with that culture, by accepting it, valuing it and learning it to a point where one can compose and be accepted that he has the gift of [poetic] composition.

According to Sengo, then, one becomes a Swahili poet by meeting the cultural and literary criteria of the Swahili people themselves!

Chiraghdin, however, raised another issue that continues to be the focus of much debate — that Swahili free verse is foreign in origin, inspired perhaps by the English poetry read in east African universities. The presupposition here is that Swahili prosodic verse is *nonforeign* and, to some, specifically "Bantu" in its origins. For example, Mayoka, in an introduction to his poetic anthology, repudiates the free verse anthologies of poets like Kezilahabi, Kahigi, and Mulokozi in the following terms:

> Katika kitabu hiki, tungo kama za Kezilahabi, Kahigi, Mulokozi na wengineo watungao tungo tutumbi zisi-

zokuwa na sanaa yoyote nimezitupa pembeni... Muundo
na mashairi yote yaliyomo kitabuni humu ni wa asili ya
Kibantu. (1986:X)

> In this book, poems like those of Kezilahabi, Kahigi,
> Mulokozi and others who produce many compositions
> devoid of any art, have been pushed aside ... the form of
> all the poems contained in this book is Bantu in origin.

This dual claim of the Swahili nationalists — that free verse is
as foreign as prosodic verse is African — naturally set off a reaction with a dual counterclaim. Pleading innocent to the charge
of succumbing to Eurocentric poetics, advocates of free verse
argue that, on the contrary, it is Swahili's prosodic verse that is
externally inspired. Prosodic poetry is seen as a symptom of
Arab cultural imperialism. Those who champion the cause of
prosodic poetry, therefore, are regarded as defenders, perhaps
unconscious ones, of a poetics rooted in Arab cultural imperialism. As Mulokozi and Kahigi claim:

> Kwa hivyo basi malenga wa Kiswahili wanaotetea vina na
> mizani hawatetei mambo ya msingi katika ushairi wa
> Kiswahili, bali wanatetea athari za kiarabu, ijapokuwa
> kinafsi sio kusudi lao. Kwa kweli wengi wanaamini kuwa
> wanachokitetea ndio "uafrika." (1979:10)

> Therefore Swahili poets who defend rhyme and meter are
> not defending any fundamentals of Swahili poetry; rather
> they are defending Arabic influences even though this is
> not their objective. In fact many believe that what they are
> defending is the "African tradition."

Proponents of free verse further argue that Swahili free verse
found its inspiration not in English poetry but in an African
and specifically Bantu poetic tradition. As Mulokozi and Kahigi
again suggest:

> Sasa je, ushairi wa mtiririko una asili ya Kizungu? Kwa
> hakika, dai hili la wanajadi lingekuwa sahihi iwapo mtindo
> wa aina hii usingekuwapo katika fasihi simulizi ya kibantu,
> ambayo ni pamoja na ile ya Kiswahili... mtindo usiofuata

vina na urari wa mizani ni wa kijadi katika fasihi ya Kiswahili na kibantu. (1979:11)

Now then, does free verse have European origins? This claim of the traditionalists would have been correct if this form did not exist in Bantu oral literature, which includes that of Swahili. . . [But] the form that follows neither rhyme nor meter is ancestral to Swahili and Bantu literature.

To these scholars, then, the shift from prosodic to free verse in Swahili poetry is part of the process of cultural decolonization, an exercise in the total Bantu reclamation of Swahili poetry from Arab appropriation.

Reactions and counterreactions have led both groups of writers to be conceptual captives of a Eurocentric cultural puritanism with each group claiming that its "brand" of Swahili poetry is more purely African than the other. The two views represent, in effect, two sides of the same coin, a coin that is both ahistorical and arbitrary. It is difficult to say when prosodic verse actually began in Swahili poetry, but there is no doubt that is was prompted, at least in part, by Swahili poets from the ranks of Swahili literati who had been inspired by Arabic poetics. With these influences Swahili poetry continued to grow, in scope and quality, *qua* Swahili poetry and *not* as the imitation of Arabic poetics.

The same can be said of Swahili free verse. There is absolutely no doubt that English free verse has been its main source of inspiration. At the same time it is a mode of poetry that is increasingly differentiating itself from its English origins, taking on a Swahili character of its own, prompting further growth of Swahili poetry, in quality and scope. It is in this connection that we agree to some considerable extent with Farouk Topan, who, in trying to explain some of the probable reasons for the emergence of Swahili free verse as a new phenomenon among members of the east African academic community, writes:

The choice of this form of composition, obviously influenced by modern English poetry, probably arises out of the desire of these young poets to react against the rigidity of the older but popular form . . . it also reflects a sense of literary challenge on a fresh mode of expression. Be that as it may, traditional scholars — staunch supporters of popular poetry — have already denounced this form as "non-Swahili." They fear that its acceptance as a bona fide form of Swahili poetry will not only dilute the composition of popular poetry but that it might even undermine it. . . . I find it difficult to accept [such] views; on the contrary, I believe that the acceptance of this modern form will enhance the status of Swahili poetry, enrich the genre, and widen the scope of its composition. (1974:176)

To recapitulate, then, the polarity in the debate on Swahili prosody seems to lie in the fact that both proponents of prosodic verse and advocates of free verse have accepted the assumption that "foreign" cultural influences are *a priori* undesirable and that we should always strive towards African cultural purity. This position, as we have suggested above, is quite Eurocentric in essence. It embodies an ahistoricity that can only lead us to artistic inertia. What is important is that such influences should not be artificially imposed from above, but should be allowed to grow organically within the body of Swahili poetry.

The debate on Swahili prosody, however, has been further "ideologized" by some advocates of free verse by invoking the notion of "feudalist decay." Meter and rhyme are now considered no more than decorative devices of a decaying feudalist order inimical to new forces of social and economic change. The first person to draw this equation was perhaps Mulokozi when he stated:

Uozo na ubaradhuli wa maisha ya kiumwinyi, hasa wakati mfumo huo unapoanza kutetereka kutokana na mabadiliko ya nguvu za jamii na uchumi, huwafanya mamwinyi, katika maisha yao ya kizembe na kifasiki, wapendelee sana mambo ya kuvutia macho na kuliwaza pua, kama vile mapambo aina aina, wanawake wazuri, nakshi na marembo ya rangi za kuvutia katika makazi na malazi yao. . . marashi na manukato, udi na ubani (na kadhalika). . . . (1975:12)

The decadence and foolishness of feudalist lifestyle, especially at a time when that order is beginning to shake due to

changes in social and economic forces, make the feudal aris-
tocrats, in their idle and immoral life, favor, very much,
things attractive to the eyes and soothing to the nose, like
various kinds of decoration, beautiful women, colorful
adornments and ornaments in their places of residence and
sleeping . . . rose water and perfumes, aromatic aloe wood
and frankincense (and so forth) . . . .

And in complete support of Mulokozi, Senkoro concludes:

Ni wazi kuwa baadhi ya washairi wetu wa Kiswahili
wanaosisitiza mno kuhusu mapambo katika maana ya
ushairi wanasisitiza tu mtazamo wa kimwinyi waliorithi
vivi hivi tu bila kutambua asili yake. (1988:7)

It is clear [then] that some of our Swahili poets who insist
on decorations in the definition of poetry are only insisting
on a feudalist perspective which they have inherited and
accepted blindly without knowing its origin.

These statements take the Swahili people — in the narrow,
ethnic sense of the term — to be the primary antagonists of free
verse; they have, therefore, been singled out for a cultural offensive coated in quasileftist acrimony. In eastern Africa it is the
Swahili society that is known for women who make that extra
effort to look beautiful, to dress attractively, to use aromatic
compounds on their bodies and dress, and so forth. It is the
appreciation of these aspects of Swahili culture, and the rhyme
and meter of its poetry, that is considered a product of the decadence, foolishness, idleness, and immorality of a decaying feudal order.

We must admit at the outset that the presumed connection
between the appreciation of beauty and behavioral decadence,
foolishness, idleness, and immorality is well beyond our conception. It seems to us that the Swahili cultural equation proposed by Mulokozi and Senkoro is merely a demonstration of
how well we have internalized colonial modes of perception.
Just as the British colonial settlers and officers once called the
Kikuyu lazy, the Kamba immoral, the Luo dirty, the African
primitive and barbaric, we have now begun to use more or less
the same subhuman labels for each other. Sadly, colonial racist

writers have inadvertently remained our mentors, and we are yet to be exorcised of the pervasive ghost of Eurocentric and colonial scholarship.

It is also simplistic to believe that we are witnessing the demise of "decadence," "foolishness," "idleness," and "immorality" in east African cultures just because the so-called feudalist order is capitulating to new social and economic forces of capitalism. The deformed capitalism in Africa, reflecting the center-periphery relations in the global economic order, has precipitated its own cultural and social problems: the "commoditization" of beauty itself, increasing sexual exploitation, and marginalization of certain sections of society, graft, blind consumerism, and so forth. If Swahili free verse, then, is one of the results of the new socio-economic forces of capitalism, and if we venture to associate free verse with capitalist culture (as Mulokozi associates prosodic verse with feudalist culture), then we are led to the fallacy that Swahili poetic development is no more than a compounding of one form of literary decadence over another!

More surprising perhaps, coming as it does from distinguished Swahili literary critics, is the notion that meter and rhyme are no more than "decorative devices" rooted in a feudalist ethos. First, meter and rhyme in poetry are by no means peculiar to a feudal culture. There are numerous precapitalist, nonfeudal cultures in Africa that have, to one degree or another, made use of rhyme and meter. Second, meter and rhyme are not merely decorative; even when composed in a written mode, Swahili prosodic verse has remained overwhelmingly oral in presentation, always subject to chanting and singing. Because of this, rhyme and meter serve as effective artistic devices and not as mere decorations. The bias that we have accepted in favor of the written word has made us blind to the oral nature of much of African verse and the place of rhyme and meter in the presentation of such verse. Finally, though free verse does not necessarily make use of rhyme and meter, it does contain other prosodic features. Swahili free verse is poetic because it embodies the unique prosodic features that make a verse poetic in the first place. Should we, too, regard these prosodic features of Swahili free verse as no more than decorative in function? This misguided line of argument, taken to its logical conclusion, leads us to question the very existence of literature as an artistic mode of expression, something that we believe Mulokozi and Senkoro did not intend to say.

Having looked at the prosodic aspect of the debate between the proponents of free verse and the Swahili poetic conservationists,[24] let us turn to the second aspect, the aspect of the language of Swahili poetry. The point of departure of the linguistic dimension of this debate is the liberalist charge that the language of Swahili prosodic verse has evolved into a mode of discourse that is alien to the linguistic world of the "common man." Linguistically, it is suggested that prosodic poetry has become the exclusive reserve of a conservative few. As Kezilahabi puts it:

> Ushairi wa Kiswahili umekuwa kwa mda mrefu mazungumzo kati ya watu wachache wauelewao au kikundi kidogo. Ipo haja ya kutelemka chini kwa watu wa kawaida na kuufanya utapakae. (Kezilahabi, 1976:xiv)

> For a long time Swahili poetry had turned into a dialogue among a few people who understand it or [members of] a small group. There is need to bring it down to [the level of] the common man and get it to spread.

But, in fact, Cory, a British resident in what was then Tanganyika, had anticipated Kezilahabi by a decade and a half. Cory had taken a liking to the popular Swahili verse that appeared in local newspapers, but he was quite bothered by the fact that he could not understand much of it despite the fact that he regarded his proficiency in Swahili as approximating that of a native speaker. He sought the assistance of educated Africans who he felt were more competent in the Swahili language. But to his dismay, he discovered that they too fared no better than he. Alarmed by this state of affairs, Cory finally remarked:

> Basi nilikuwa na wasiwasi, maana mashairi hayapasi kabisa kutungwa kama kwamba mashairi ni maarifa ya kufahamiwa na watu wachache walioelimika sana bali yapasa yafahamiwe na watu wote wenye maarifa ya kusoma na kuandika, pia na wengine wasiokuwa nayo. Labda mimi sikufahamu kwa sababu sikuwa na maarifa ya

117

kutosha, au labda wale niliowachagua kunisaidia hawaku-
fahamu vilevile. Lakini kwa vyo vyote, nina hakika ya kuwa
Mwafrika asiye na elimu nyingi ya Kiswahili haelewi wala
kupendezwa na mashairi mengi ya Kiswahili yanay-
otungwa siku hizi. (Cory, 1958:v)

So I became concerned, because poetry should not be
composed as if it is esoteric; rather it should be understood
by all literate people, as well as by those who are not literate. It is possible that I did not understand because my
knowledge was insufficient, or perhaps the people I chose
to assist me were also not knowledgeable. But, whatever
the case, I am sure any African who is not highly educated
in the Swahili language cannot understand or appreciate
many current Swahili poems.

Cory regarded this as essentially a linguistic problem, which he
attributed to the impact of Arabic poetics on Swahili poetry. As
a way of remedying the situation, therefore, Cory suggests that
Swahili poetry must seek a break from the Arab-Islamic tradition and allow itself to come under European influence (Cory,
1958:vii). And as a step in that direction, this European, Cory,
himself produced what may be regarded as the first anthology
of Swahili free verse.

To recapitulate, proponents of free verse seem to agree that
the language of Swahili verse in the prosodic tradition has
tended to be linguistically alienated from "the people" due to
its *semantic opacity*. An impression has thus been created that
some specialized knowledge has become necessary if one is to
discover meaning in the prosodic poetry. If this is true, then,
what are some of the more specific linguistic features of
prosodic poetry that may be held accountable for a level of
semantic opacity that has rendered it inaccessible except to a
select few? It is to a discussion of these specific linguistic attributes of prosodic poetry that we must now turn.

The proponents of free verse have raised two linguistic objec-
tions to Swahili poetry of the classical pre-twentieth century
type. The first objection refers to the frequency of linguistic
Arabisms regarded by them as evidence of a colonial mentality. Mulokozi, commenting on this syndrome in pre-twentieth
century Swahili epic *tenzi* poems, writes:

118

This type of colonial mentality is, of course, reflected in the language. Some of the tenzi written at this time are so full of Arabic words and borrowings that it becomes impossible for one not conversant with Arabic to get their full meaning. (Mulokozi, 1975:52)

Shariff, one of the authors of this present text (1988:208-212), has responded to the sentiments expressed by Mulokozi by appealing to the notion of linguistic register. Observing that linguistic Arabisms are found mostly in poems with a religious theme, Shariff argues that it is natural that Arabisms would have a special place in Swahili religious poetry given the status of the Arabic language in Islam. Sound as Shariff's argument may be, however, it tells only part of the story as it fails to account for Arabisms in nonreligious poetry.

The second objection rests upon the supposed use of "difficult words" in the language of prosodic poetry. It has been suggested by Senkoro, for example, that this aspect of poetic language is the result of the "bourgeois" notion of the poet as a prophet or as a human deity:

Imani hii, ambayo imeenea hasa katika nchi za kibepari ambako mwanasanaa ni mtu maalumu asiye mmoja wa watu anaoandika juu yao, imepata nafasi kubwa sana katika kuipotosha nadharia ya Kiswahili. Kwa kufuatana na nadharia hii, baadhi ya washairi wa Kiswahili wameshikilia kutumia maneno magumu magumu. . . . (Senkoro, 1988:6)

This belief which is most prevalent in capitalist countries where the artist is a special being and not among the people about whom he/she is writing, has played a major role in distorting the entire perspective of Swahili poetry. Following this view, some Swahili poets have insisted on using difficult words. . . .

It is not quite clear what Senkoro means by "difficult words." The phrase seems to include, but is not restricted to, linguistic Arabisms and generally seems to refer to lexical items that are not within the purview of the average Swahili speaker. The term, then, would include words that are jargonistic, archaic, and those confined to specific regional dialects, all of which are found in prosodic Swahili poetry.

Senkoro's claim that this linguistic trend in Swahili poetry emerged partly as a result of the impact of some "bourgeois" notion of the artist is hardly justifiable in view of what we know about the biographies of the more prominent "traditional" Swahili poets. Virtually all of these poets have risen to this elite status by the power of their artistry and not by virtue of any exposure to intellectual paradigms of the North. Unlike their university counterparts, the more prominent traditionalist poets are more akin to Gramsci's "organic intellectuals," having arisen from the ranks of the people and not apart from them. Insofar as the Swahili community itself is concerned, these, and not the composers of free verse, are the people's poets, inaccessible as their compositions may at times appear to be. They are products of the Swahili intellectual soil and not of northern cultural infusion into east Africa.

The specific linguistic features that constitute a point of contention in Swahili poetry then are best seen, not in terms of a predetermined northern paradigm, but historically in terms of the development of Swahili prosody specifically and the Swahili language in general. It is reasonable to presume that, in the pre-Liyongo era, Swahili verse was not bound by rules of meter and rhyme. At this juncture the compositions were exclusively oral and rendered in the respective "primary Swahili dialects" of the composers, i.e., in those dialects that existed prior to the spread of the language beyond its "original" coastal borders, and certainly prior to the emergence of what has come to be known as "standard" Swahili.

In the meantime the Swahili people continued their historical interaction and interrelation with Arab, Persian, and other African traders and settlers. Expectedly this African-Arab equation eventually had its own impact on the development of the Swahili language and its poetry. We have already discussed the more pronounced features of this impact in the previous chapter. So we shall simply summarize them here. These include:

1. The development of writing, using a Swahili diagraph of Arabic, i.e., a modified version of Arabic orthography. Writing now opened up the way for a degree of experi-

mentation in poetic form that was not easily possible in the oral mode.

2. Swahili exposure to Arabic prosody. This external influence and the stimulus of writing complemented the internal dynamics of the Swahili language and literature to generate a Swahili prosody based on meter and rhyme. By the nineteenth century a great classical tradition in meter and rhyme had been firmly established on Swahili soil. This classical tradition so captured the imagination of the Swahili that it has continued to influence Swahili poets, linguistically and functionally, to this day. Linguistic items and forms that were once in common use, but are now obsolete, have continued to appear in the poetry of Swahili traditionalist artists.

3. The expansion of Islam to the point where the religion became one of the distinctive features of Swahili identity. This affected the linguistic destiny of Swahili poetry in two ways:

    a. The sacredness attributed to the Arabic language in Islam influenced the use of unassimilated linguistic Arabisms in the Swahili language and subsequently in Swahili poetry.

    b. With the religion came the scholastic tradition, and the island of Lamu on the northern coast of Kenya came to establish itself as the seat of Swahili-Islamic learning. In this way the Swahili dialect of Lamu came into prominence as the more "cultural dialect" affecting both Swahili religious and poetic discourse, especially in Kenya. This tendency was further boosted by the emergence of master-poets from within the ranks of the Lamu Muslim scholars composing in the Lamu dialect of Swahili. The use of linguistic Arabisms and Lamu dialect forms came to be most pronounced in religious poetry; but, to a lesser degree perhaps, they also influenced secular Swahili poetry.

By the time the Germans and the British arrived in east Africa, therefore, they "discovered" a Swahili poetry that was predominantly prosodic (in rhyme and meter), composed in the respective primary Swahili dialects of the poets who sometimes made extensive use of unassimilated linguistic Arabisms, of linguistic "archaisms" from the classical poetic tradition, and of some items of Lamu dialect, whenever deemed beneficial to the aesthetic quality of the compositions. These features became part and parcel of the wider aesthetic norm of Swahili poetry, a norm shared by the composers as well as the audience that in most cases included the average, *common* Swahili person. And this is a norm that many continue to hold on to in the Swahili community.

The Arab-Islamic impact had managed to spread Swahili beyond its original borders, but the language played no more than an auxiliary function among those non-Swahili who acquired it in the process of trade. The contact with the Germanic-Christian civilization in the nineteenth century, however, prompted new dynamics in the development of Swahili language and literature:

1. Colonialism introduced new institutions and set in motion a major flux of demographic and other forces. In the process the school, the church, the economic, and political arenas became new venues for the acquisition of the language. If the Arab-Islamic impact initially helped to spread the use of Swahili at the marketplace, the Germanic-Christian influence helped diversify its function among non-Swahili to other spheres of social life. In the meantime, especially in Tanzania, Swahili identity itself became politicized and became more inclusive. In Tanzania today a Swahili person has come to mean virtually anyone who is African in origin. The school, the church, and the media also came to play their role in exposing those who spoke Swahili as a second or an additional language to Swahili literature.

2. A standard Swahili based on the Zanzibar dialect was established. If the Lamu or Mombasa dialects of Swahili were developing into standard norms for religious-cultural reasons (which of course had politico-economic foundations), this process was now subverted by the introduction of this later standard norm from above, specifically during the colonial period. Varieties of this standard norm became the Swahili of the school, the churches, and the media, and the poetry of non-native speakers of the language came to be composed in these historically more

recent Swahili varieties.

3. The study of English literature in schools had the added effect of exposing the east African to a new kind of poetry which was later to inspire experimentation in Swahili free verse and abstract metaphors.

The end result of all this was the expansion of the social basis of Swahili literary culture in such a way that the intellectual stratum that could now produce the new generation of poets came to be comprised much more of those who spoke it as an additional language than those who arose from the "traditional" Swahili ethnic group. This demographic shift coincided, then, with the birth of a new aesthetic norm that, in some respects, seems to be in conflict with the more "traditional" Swahili aesthetic norm. The gradually diminishing extremes of this conflict are represented, at one pole, by poets who believe they are composing for the narrow group of traditional common Swahili, who have been and continue to be exposed to their respective primary dialects, to Arabisms, archaisms, and "Lamuisms," and, at the other pole, by poets who believe they compose for the wider group of *common* non-Swahili, who have been exposed to none of these linguistic peculiarities of the traditional Swahili.

A conjuncture of social, political, and economic forces has since then been acting on the east African community that promises to decrease the linguistic gap between prosodic poetry of the classical type and free verse. For example, even among the most conservationist of Swahili poets, considerations of educational-cum-market conditions have begun to have a definite impact on the linguistic aspect of their prosodic verse. The largest market for Swahili written verse in east Africa is the secondary school, and publishers are willing to produce poetry that usually caters to this audience. But precisely because the school favors standard Swahili, or variations of it, poets are increasingly being pressured to shift to the standard norm if they hope to have their manuscripts published and used in schools.

Whatever the case, it is against the presumed linguistic position of the traditionalist poets that the proponents of free verse felt compelled to "rebel." There has been the feeling that a major linguistic and prosodic revolution is required if Swahili poetics is to be liberated from the fetters of the classical tradition and allowed its full potential for growth and development. Linguistically, this revolution has been seen in terms of a break from the "poetic diction of old" and greater use of the "common language of the people." As Kezilahabi declares in the introduction to his poetic anthology *Kichomi*:

> Jambo ninalotaka kuleta katika ushairi wa Kiswahili ni utumiaji wa lugha ya kawaida, lugha itumiwayo na watu katika mazungumzo yao ya kila siku ... Mapinduzi haya ya kutotumia vina na kutumia lugha ya kawaida ya watu yanatokea katika ushairi wa nchi mbalimbali. Nami nime-fanya hivyo, siyo kuwaiga, lakini kwa kuwa naamini kwamba mapinduzi ya aina hii ni hatua moja kubwa mbele katika ushairi wa Kiswahili. (Kezilahabi, 1974:xii-iv)

> What I would like to introduce in Swahili poetry is the use of a common language; the language used by people in their normal daily conversations. . . . This revolution of not using rhyme and using the common language of people has taken place in the poetry of many nations. And I have done so, not to imitate them, but because I believe that this kind of revolution is a major step ahead in Swahili poetry.

In a sense, then, Kezilahabi's position constitutes an introduction of the Wordsworthian debate to African soil, the launching of the Wordsworthian linguistic revolution in Swahiliphone Africa. This supposed linguistic revolution in Swahili poetry has meant a shift away from more localized dialects of Swahili (like Kiamu) to a dialect of wider communication, i.e., standard Swahili, a virtual rejection of "archaisms" and unassimilated Arabisms, and shunning, to a large extent, the use of the long-established poetic practice of lexical contraction (hitherto used mainly to fulfill metric requirements). This revolution as Kezilahabi sees it, is supposed to make Swahili verse less obscure, more semantically accessible, thereby taking it closer to "the people."

Of course, "linguistic proximity to the people" is a relative notion depending on the poet's intended audience. Native speakers of the Kimvita dialect (spoken in Mombasa) and Kiamu dialect (spoken in Lamu), who have grown up with the classical poetic tradition, are likely to be less alienated from the poetry of Nabhany, for example, than would be the case with non-Swahili, noncoastal Kenyans. Part of the linguistic problem, then, actually boils down to the kinds of audiences for which the two schools of poets compose. And as the traditionalist poets' own conception of their audience expands to include non-native speakers of Swahili, their language is likely to be affected in the direction of greater penetrability at the level of diction.

When all is said and done, however, the proposed shift in Swahili poetry has not been viewed favorably by members of the conservationist school. Their reaction is not so much against the use of standard Swahili and the restriction of Swahili diction to more current sources. After all, such poetry has existed even prior to the emergence of free verse. Rather, the proponents of prosodic verse have been reacting to the treatment of this linguistic sentiment as a matter of both ideology and policy. The freedom to compose in the more traditional poetic idiom that the Swahili poet had always enjoyed was now under threat, and it was felt that that idiom had to be protected if Swahili poetry was not to end up feeble and stunted. According to Chiraghdin, for example, accepting this emergent poetic form in Swahili literature would imply the following:

> . . . Kanuni zote za ushairi wa Kiswahili zitakuwa pindu pindu, vina vitakuwa havijulikani mwanzo havijulikani mwisho, na lugha yenyewe itakuwa chapwa au kuzidi. Na tungo hizo zikikubaliwa kuwa ni mashairi basi ushairi wa Kiswahili utakuwa umeanguka kitakotako. (1974:14)

> . . . All the fundamentals of Swahili poetry will be overturned, rhyme will lose its place and identity, and the language itself will be stale or even worse. And if these are regarded as Swahili poems then Swahili poetry will have fallen flat on its behind.

Elsewhere, Chiraghdin makes an impassioned appeal against confining Swahili poetry to a standard linguistic norm for fear of reducing its aesthetic potency (1974:x-xii).

To the Swahili nationalists, therefore, the pan-dialectization of Swahili poetry and the confinement of its poetic diction to the linguistic here and now could only amount to the dilution of Swahili's aesthetic punch. The two poles of the debate around the question of poetic diction, therefore, seem hardly reconcilable.

Sengo, one of the defenders of the prosodic tradition, seems to be of the opinion that this entire "hullabaloo" boils down to one thing: that the advocates of free verse are linguistically ill-equipped to compose in what he asserts as the more linguistically demanding, traditional, prosodic mode. According to Sengo:

> Siri moja ambayo ni kubwa katika utunzi wa mashairi au tenzi za Kiswahili ni kuimanya lugha kwa undani wake. Siri hii yathibitishwa na mtaalamu mmoja, naye anasema: "Kadiri mtunzi alivyotopea katika lugha ya Kiswahili ndivyo kadiri atakavyopata wepesi katika kazi yake na kutiririka nayo kama maji ya mto. . . ."

> Na pengine hii ndiyo siri inayowafunga hao wataalamu wa kundi la kwanza. Nafikiri wengi wao wangependa sana kuwa watunzi mahiri wa mashairi na tenzi za Kiswahili na kwa hivyo kushiriki katika kuendeleza na kukuza ushairi wa Kiswahili na lugha ya Kiswahili kwa jumla; lakini kwa kuwa hawanacho kipawa hicho inawawia vigumu kutimiza azma yao. (1978:vi)

> One major secret in composing Swahili poetry is to have a deep knowledge of the language. This secret is affirmed by a certain scholar who says: "The more one is steeped in the Swahili language, the greater will be his facility in accomplishing his mission and flow with it like the river. . . ."

> And probably this is the secret that constrains the scholars of the first group [advocates of free verse]. I think many of them would have liked to be skillful composers of Swahili poetry, thereby participating in developing Swahili poetry and the Swahili language in general; but because they do not have the [linguistic] capacity, it has become difficult for them to accomplish their objective.

While there is little doubt that an extensive knowledge of the language, of its vocabulary and metaphor, is a tremendous asset to a poet, Sengo's statement still begs the question: Should unassimilated linguistic Arabisms and archaisms be considered part of one's competence in the language of modern Swahili poetry? If his answer to this question is in the affirmative, then the charge that prosodic verse has become a form of specialized communication for a select few may not be altogether far-fetched.

The linguistic revolution intended by the advocates of free verse is by no means confined to the level of diction. It is also supposed to encompass the level of metaphor. Some members of the liberalist school seem to regard prosodic poetry as wanting in metaphor. This alleged metaphoric deficiency of prosodic verse is in turn deemed non-Bantu to the extent that "traditional" Bantu verse is rich in metaphor. Kezilahabi notes:

> ... mashairi ya wahenga wetu yalikuwa yakiweka mkazo zaidi juu ya mafumbo kuliko vina na mizani. Kwa hivyo uelewaji wa shairi ulikuwa uwezo wa kufumbua fumbo.(1974:xiv)

> ... the poetry of our ancestors used to place more emphasis on metaphor than on rhyme and meter. Therefore the comprehension of a poem involved the unpacking of a metaphor.

And it is purportedly from this Bantu source that Kezilahabi himself sought guidance and inspiration for the metaphoric language used in his collection of poems, *Kichomi*. Topan (1974:186), on the other hand, discusses the special metaphoric quality of Swahili free verse in terms of "symbolic imagery" whose aesthetic appeal lies in its potential for multiple interpretation. For Topan, too, this is an attribute that is more characteristic of free verse than it is of prosodic verse.

But in the case of both Kezilahabi and Topan, it is difficult to know exactly what they mean, since they have been less than explicit about the problem in relation to prosodic verse. Both metaphoric language and "symbolic imagery" are by no means artistic devices newly introduced into Swahili literature by the pioneering design of free verse. It is possible, however, that the metaphoric language in free verse has tended towards greater abstractness and ambiguity than the metaphoric language in prosodic verse.

In recapitulation, then, whereas advocates of free verse find prosodic verse both inaccessible in its diction and less symbolic in its metaphor, defenders of the prosodic tradition seem to regard the proposed language of free verse as wanting in expressiveness and poetic power.

Between 1981 and 1982, one of the present authors, Alamin Mazrui, had the opportunity to teach courses in Swahili literature at Kenyatta University and at the University of Nairobi in Kenya. In the field of poetry, studied were written verse composed both in prosodic (in the classical tradition) and free verse. And, indeed, almost invariably, students found the diction of prosodic verse less penetrable than that of free verse. It is no wonder, then, that many anthologies of prosodic Swahili poetry contain glossaries to guide the reader. For second or third language speakers of Swahili, "unassimilated Arabisms" seemed to be at the top of the hierarchy of linguistic impenetrability, followed by "archaisms" that were followed, in turn, by lexical contractions. In general, however, once the students had the opportunity to fathom the meaning of the specific lexical items they found problematic, the poems became immediately accessible. They seemed to experience no problem in appreciating and dealing with the metaphor used in many a prosodic verse.

The situation seemed quite the reverse in the case of free verse. Students were generally comfortable with its diction and rarely did they have to refer to glossaries or dictionaries for the literal meaning of words. Despite this, however, free verse tended to be semantically less accessible at the level of metaphor. Under a modernist aesthetics, interpretation of metaphorical and figurative language is deemed part and parcel of the process of literary appreciation. But experience in Swahili free verse has often been one in which literary appreciation becomes subsidiary to meeting the intellectual challenge offered by its poetic metaphor. This state of affairs may, of course, have a lot to do with the novelty of free verse in the Swahili literary tradition.

In their quest for a new poetic order, therefore, poets com

posing in free verse seem to have replaced one kind of linguistic impenetrability, that of diction, with another kind, that of metaphor. They seem to have shifted from one level of semantic inaccessibility to another, perhaps more elusive, level. Ironically, what was intended to be "the common language of the people" in Swahili free verse has turned out to be as incomprehensible as, if not more so than, the "specialized language" of classical poetry. If prosodic poetry has been accused of being a restricted dialogue between members of a small group of literary conservationists or "organic intellectuals," free verse can now be said to have assumed the character of specialized discourse among a small circle of "inorganic intellectuals" (to use Gramsci's terms).

Taken to its logical conclusion, the linguistic position of the advocates of free verse is actually quite unrealistic. To expect the language of poetry to be in conformity with the "language used by people in their normal daily conversation," as Kezilahabi puts it, is to expect language to go against its very nature, to turn against its inherent character of dynamic variability. Language is a highly differentiated system, and to exclude poetry from this general sociolinguistic rule is to operate in the realm of the unreal. Accepting, then, that the language of poetry will take its own course of development, poets and critics concerned about Swahili poetry's accessibility must strive towards both more penetrable diction as well as penetrable metaphor.

In the meantime, however, we must remember that in terms of Swahili identity, specifically, the value of poetic language goes well beyond poetry. Poetic language becomes the ideal by which rhetorical speech in every day communication is judged. As Ali Mazrui comments:

> There is a school of thought in English poetry, represented by such people as Wordsworth and Coleridge, to the effect that poetry should approximate the ordinary language of conversation. But in Swahili culture there is a school of thought which would argue that ordinary conversation should try to approximate the elegant language of poetry. Those poems to the editor in Tanzanian newspapers, poems of dialogue, are part of this tradition. (1986:244-45)

As much as we would like to see a more accessible diction and metaphor in Swahili poetry, therefore, we cannot aim for a total conjunction of poetic and conversational language. For such a conjunction would not only be a negation of poetry itself, but also, if the conjunction is made in the direction of conversational language, it would constitute a reversal of Swahili linguistic values as well.[25]

In recapitulation, then, we have seen how colonialism and its aftermath introduced new criteria for judging literary quality in the world of Swahili literature. The motives for this aesthetic imposition were sometimes more explicitly colonial (as in the case of Mbotela's *Uhuru wa Watumwa*), but, more often, they had to do with the wider Eurocentric arrogance that regards European achievements as models for the rest of the world. These politics of aesthetics ultimately came to explode into a major controversy with specific regard to Swahili poetry.

Of all the literary genres, the Swahili seem to have placed special value on their poetry. Among the many features that have been used to determine the quality of poetic composition, meter and rhyme have been regarded as indispensable. The emergence of English-inspired free verse, then, was seen as an open violation of the aesthetic standards that had hitherto been operating among the Swahili people. More significantly, however, it was seen as an attempt to *dispossess* the Swahili people of an important expression of their collective consciousness and identity. To some extent, the attempt to treat modern free verse in Swahili as a foreign mode of composition is part of a wider struggle to keep the various parameters of Swahili identity intact in a politico-economic context in which the Swahili people feel marginalized and their identity threatened. It is partly against this background that the Swahili nationalists' response to free verse must be understood.

EPILOGUE
THE SWAHILI DISPOSSESSED

 the last four chapters we have tried to demonstrate that there has been a serious misrepresentation of Swahili identity at the levels of ethnicity, language, and literature. The dominance of a Eurocentric paradigm of ethnic identity, the various misconceptions about the genesis of the Swahili language, the lopsided interpretations of Swahili literature and Swahili literary history, and the external imposition of new standards of Swahili literary quality, all those have combined to undermine the very foundations of Swahili identity. The cumulative effect of the line of inquiry about Swahili ethnicity, language, and literature surveyed in the preceding chapters, therefore, has been to further problematize the collective identity of Swahili people. As intimated at various points in our discussion so far, this seeming "fuzziness" about Swahili identity has sometimes had certain implications both at the domestic and international levels. And it is the politico-economic dimension of these implications that we shall attempt to clarify in this conclusion.

The Swahili have sometimes been recognized as *victors* in their historical contribution to one of the most dynamic sociocultural systems in indigenous Africa. Their early exposure to the universalist religion of Islam, their participation in a flourishing transcontinental trade, the internationalization of their language, and the absorptive capacity of their identity were all instrumental, with other factors, in making the Swahili a major universalizing factor in east Africa.

More frequently, the Swahili have been seen also as *villains*. They have been producers of a language that some regard as threatening to other African languages in its expansionist propensity. And their previous association with the east African slave trade has often been given prominence as a historical feature of Swahili villainy.

Less appreciated, perhaps, have been the Swahili as *victims* in the crucible of east African history. One of Africa's most universalizing socio-cultural groups now seems to be in danger of being crucified at the altar of east Africa's neocolonial politics. But in what ways can the Swahili be regarded as victims in the contemporary politics of east Africa? And what have been some of the domestic and international implications of this seeming victimization? What have been some of the manifestations of the Swahili decline from major actor to a mere pawn in the arena of east Africa's political economy?

Given the small numerical size of the Swahili people, it may not be wholly unjustified to suggest that there is today what might rightly be called a Swahili diaspora, a people dispersed across several continents including Africa, Asia, Europe, and the Americas. Only with some minor exaggeration is it said that one would not be lost in cities as far apart as Nairobi (Kenya), Muscat (Oman), and Toronto (Canada) if one's linguistic proficiency is restricted to the Swahili tongue. Sensing their shared political destiny, some of these people have come to call themselves the *muhajirina*, the "exiles." In using this particular metaphor they have thus come to compare themselves with the pioneering Muslims who, fearing political persecution, had to abandon their homes in Mecca to seek refuge in Medina. Among these *muhajirina* the feeling abounds that their common destiny is not at all unrelated to their ethnic identity, or, as the perpetrators of Swahili disenfranchisement would like to believe, their lack of identity. Their sole crime, they seem to believe, has been to attempt to "monopolize" the label Swahili, a label of identity that others insist is without a people or for all the people.

The *muhajirina* have a long history that goes back to 1964 when there was an exodus of Zanzibar Swahili, especially those with Arab "blood," to other parts of the world. It was in Zanzibar that the colonially induced muddle in Swahili identity first came to have politically calamitous ramifications. Prior to the sixteenth-century Portuguese invasion, Zanzibar was a

Swahili town in the creole sense of the word, having further absorbed people of other African and non-African origins. It was a Swahili *kabila* of Zanzibar, forming a composite whole that, nonetheless, had internal groupings like the Wahadimu, Waunguja, Watumbatu, Wapemba, Wamakunduchi, and so forth. "Aliens" settled there, in time discarded their "alienness," and became full-fledged members of the Swahili *kabila* of Zanzibar.

Until the first wave of European invasion, Zanzibar was an independent and sovereign Swahili city-state with its own mode of governance and administration. The first European invaders of the Swahili coast were, of course, the Portuguese. For over three hundred years, from about the beginning of the sixteenth century, the Portuguese invasions continued to disturb the status quo in a series of military offensives and counteroffensives that also involved other Swahili states. Eventually, the Swahili, with many of their towns plundered and some burned down to the ground by the Portuguese, sought the assistance of the Omani Arabs, and jointly suc-ceeded in bringing Portuguese rule to an end. In return for that assistance, the Sultans of Oman were recognized as suzerains of the Swahili coast. This ultimately led to the estab-lishment, in 1832, of Zanzibar as the capital of the Omani sul-tanate. In the course of time, however, the links with Oman came to an end, and by 1895 Zanzibar had become a British protectorate with an Arab constitutional monarch who had no executive or administrative powers. For all practical pur-poses Zanzibar had become a British colony like any other British colony in Africa, with the British deposing and "crown-ing" the sultans at will.

But just as they did in several other parts of Africa, British colonial functionaries soon sowed seeds of discord in Zanzibar, polarizing its composite Swahili society along the now familiar Arab-African axis. By the early 1960s this artifi-cially induced rift had caused some civil trauma, the kind of strife that would bedevil many other African nations in their early phases of independence, or as in the case of the Republic of South Africa today, in the period immediately preceding independence. What had started as, and continued to be, a multiracial society was now forced by the dynamics of colonial politics to develop a false sense of racial consciousness concerning its own internal structure.

On January 11, 1964, what came to be known as the Zanzibar revolution was launched. In essence, this was the first class-based revolutionary attempt of its kind in postcolonial Africa. It was an initiative intended to bring an end to class privileges in a multiracial society through the establishment of a socialist order. Both the protagonists and the antagonists of the revolution were Swahili in the broad multiracial ethnic sense of the word. But as soon as the revolution had taken off the ground two factors intervened to derail it from its socialist path and give it a racist twist intended to retain a capitalist preeminence.

One factor was the African outer-group presence in Zanzibar. For quite a while the flourishing economy of Zanzibar had attracted many African migrant workers from what was then Tanganyika, Uganda, Kenya, Malawi, and Mozambique. Many of these had been subjects of British (and Portuguese) racist politics elsewhere and came to Zanzibar with their own stereotypes about, and prejudices against, the Swahili. The overplay of the Arab dimension of Swahili identity, the association of Islam with Arabness, and of both with slavery, the colonial categorization of Arabs as non-native, all combined in the mind of the African migrant worker to make him regard himself as having more of a right on the African island of Zanzibar than a significant section of the native population. These non-Swahili, non-Zanzibari Africans found it expedient to capitalize on the colonially induced polarization between Swahili with some Arab ancestry on the one hand, and Swahili with African and Shirazi (Persian) ancestry on the other, in pursuit of their own group interest. Blinded by the anti-Islamic venom that had long been cultivated by the Euro-Christian colonial ideology, the non-Zanzibaris saw the revolution as a means of gaining the privileges of the native population of Zanzibar. To these people, who constituted a small but politically significant proportion of the population in Zanzibar, the enemy was not a particular class of capitalists, but the Swahili body politic as a whole, especially in its highly exaggerated Arab dimension. It was probably this that motivated the likes of John Okello.[26]

The second intervening factor was Anglo-American imperialism. Those were the days when the United States government would do virtually anything to counteract the infusion of communist tendencies in Africa. The U.S. government felt compelled to intervene and derail the socialist attempt in Zanzibar. Capitalizing on the anti-Arab sentiments generated mainly by non-Zanzibaris, including John Okello and his followers, the American propaganda machine began rolling. Hoping to influence "the players" away from a socialist orientation, Anglo-American media began humming the anti-Arab tune, trying to persuade the Zanzibaris and the rest of the world that what was in process was in fact an anti-Arab revolution. At the same time the American CIA was involved in more covert action to eliminate all possibilities of socialist success in Zanzibar. In fact, it was on the CIA-inspired ideology of destroying the socialist foundations of the Zanzibar revolution that Tanzania was finally erected.[27]

The British propaganda of an "Arab threat" in Zanzibar was also partly prompted by its conflict with Egypt. Under Gamal Abdel Nasser, Egypt had emerged into a leading proponent of African liberation from European and American imperialism. It gave explicit moral and material support to several liberation movements in Africa including the Mau Mau and the Kenya African National Union (KANU) in Kenya. Due to its leftist inclinations, Egypt was also seen as an African extension of the communist threat. Egyptian support of the nationalist aspirations of Zanzibari people, therefore, gave Anglo-American imperialism further cause to use the anti-Arab campaign in Zanzibar politics as an offensive against communism.

In the meantime, the poison that had been injected by a section of non-Swahili African migrants and by Anglo-American propaganda had succeeded in unleashing a monumental reign of terror in Zanzibar. This racial poison led to a blind arbitrariness, turning sibling against sibling, child against parent, neighbor against neighbor. Indiscriminate killings and raping, mass arrest and detention, kangaroo courts and executions, all combined to make many Arabs and Swahili of Zanzibar flee for their lives and security. The confusion about Swahili identity that was prompted by European colonial politics had thus generated forced exile, a massive Swahili exodus and created the beginnings of a Swahili diaspora. The *muhajirina* had thus been born on the eve of the first and only Swahili postcolonial state in Africa, short-lived as it may have been. But the birth of the *muhajirina* also meant, for better or worse, the death of the first potential scientific socialist experiment in Africa.

The events surrounding the Zanzibar revolution generated fears that the Swahili would be further marginalized in what came to be known as mainland Tanzania. These fears were certainly not without foundation. The Tanganyika army mutiny of January 20, 1964, for example, is said to have been on the verge of turning into the same kind of genocidal slaughter against "Arabs" and Muslims that flamed across Zanzibar (Cohen, 1966:167). To what extent, then, have these fears been confirmed since the birth of Tanzania? As indicated in the first chapter, however, Swahili identity has itself been undergoing a rapid demographic expansion in mainland Tanzania due to a conjucture of several factors. As a result, it is not easy to talk of Swahili marginality in that region of east Africa. On the other hand, there have been strong claims of Muslim (which includes Swahili) underrepresentation in Tanzania's public affairs. In the final analysis, therefore, Swahili marginality in mainland Tanzania may be subsumed under a broader marginality of the country's Muslim population.

The centrality of individuals like the current President, Ali Hassan Mwinyi, and the OAU Secretary General, Salim Ahmed Salim, who have moved through the ranks to the highest echelons of power has sometimes been invoked to argue against claims of Swahili marginality in Tanzania. But we should not forget that both of these politicians come from Zanzibar, and their rise to power has been prompted less by a process of widening Swahili political participation than by the dictates of the union of Zanzibar and Tanganyika. If the initiative of Julius Nyerere, the country's first president, to establish the federation of Tanzania were to endure, it had to be demonstrated that Zanzibar Swahili enjoyed at least a semblance of equality of opportunities in the newly constituted polity.

But even with regard to the Zanzibar Swahili population, there is evidence of mounting fears of collective dispossession wrought by the islands' union with Tanganyika. Over the last couple of years there have been strong protests in Zanzibar against the federation. Inhabitants of Zanzibar have sometimes

expressed quasinationalist sentiments that border on seces-
sionism. In the process, revivalist tendencies around major symbols of Swahili identity, like Islam and the Swahili language in
its primary dialectal forms, have reemerged with increasing
militancy. From the pulpits of mosques to the stages of *taarabu*
gatherings, "pro-independence" pronouncements in Zanzibar
have become legion. The protestors have been spurred by the
feeling that the union of Tanganyika and Zanzibar was, in fact,
a conspiracy of a sort intended to thwart the economic and
political potential of the Zanzibar Swahili. The islands' own
progress and development, it has often been suggested, have
been sacrificed to cater to the needs of the "other" partner in the
federation and, more specifically, to the needs of the non-
Swahili population of mainland Tanzania. Under the circumstances, Tanzania's attempts to "nationalize" Swahili identity
has sometimes been interpreted as further evidence of a silent
policy of marginalization of Zanzibaris.

Be that as it may, the implications of the confusion about
Swahili identity that were manifested in the immediate aftermath of Zanzibar's independence unfolded somewhat more
gradually in other parts of east Africa, especially in Kenya. The
dynamics of neocolonialism had begun to deform the economics and politics of the region in very concrete ways. The dominance of foreign capital in the more productive sectors of the
economy, in the manufacturing and commercial sectors in particular, had two effects on the embryonic African bourgeoisie.
First, it tended to restrict them to economic areas whose mode
bordered on primitive accumulation. The embryonic bourgeoisie were thus quickly transformed, not into captains of commerce and industry, but into traders of the intermediary type
and speculators of real estate.

Second, and subsequent to the economic marginalization of
the embryonic bourgeoisie in the global capitalist order, neocolonialism helped turn the east African state into an instrument of accumulation. Even to invest in economic enterprises
of the intermediary type the embryonic bourgeoisie, of course,
needed capital. One way of building their capital was to use the
institutions of the state for purposes of accumulation. In east
Africa, as in many other African countries, therefore, top state
and government functionaries have also tended to be its bour-

geoisie, and terms like "bureaucratic" bourgeoisie, "govern-
ing" (as opposed to ruling) classes came to be developed to
depict precisely this convergence between economic and political powers in neocolonial Africa. Whatever the case, this accu-
mulative function of the state, in conjunction with other factors,
has often resulted in kleptocracy, in thievery as part of "governance."

In a neocolony where resources and opportunities are limited,
these kleptocratic interests, these economic interests of the bourgeoisie that are fused with the state, again in conjunction with
other forces, may give rise to two other tendencies. The first is
the autocratic tendency, the concentration of political power in
the executive president of the country, in the head of a state that
has sometimes been described as corporatist. Under this system, civil liberties and human rights, often enshrined in the
constitution, are violated under a misguided developmentalist
rhetoric that requires its citizens to be unmindful of "politics"
for the sake of the nation's economic "development." But the
real function of this autocracy is that the suspension of "political" rights and liberties, if accepted as the nation's ideology,
would allow the bourgeoisie to pursue their kleptocratic interests without accountability.

The second tendency that may result from a kleptocratic system is ethnocracy, the ethnic orientation in managing (or perhaps mismanaging) the affairs of the nation. Economic
insecurities that are typical of the neocolonial countries often
lead to ethnic competitiveness and ethnic scramble for the small
and diminishing "national cake." All things being equal then,
power and privileges are distributed by the autocrat in con-
centric circles of kith and kin. To some extent, then, the ethnic
compatriots of the autocrat may constitute a privileged group
in the national population. If the president, for example, is
Swahili, then, all things being equal, the job of an office mes-
senger is more likely to go to a Swahili candidate than, say, a
Kalenjin candidate. The opposite side of this ethnocratic dimension, then, would be the placement of the average members of
ethnic groups other than that of the autocrat in an underprivileged position. Under a Swahili ethnocracy, for example, the
Giriama, the Gikuyu, the Luo, and so forth will all tend to be
underprivileged relative to the Swahili.

Different ethnic groups in a neocolony, however, need not be underprivileged to the same degree. For a variety of reasons that we need not go into here, ethnic "underprivilegedness" can be quite relative. Nor is the ethnic hierarchy of privileges rigid and static. Rather it is always in a state of flux, some elements filtering downwards, others moving upwards on the basis of a nation's changing political dynamics. The underprivileged of yesterday may become the privileged of tomorrow and visa versa. Just as ethnicity is both relative and dynamic, therefore, the assets and liabilities accorded to it may also be relative and changing. Nor is it incompatible with interests and practices of ethnocracy to co-opt an elite from the underprivileged ethnic group into systems of power and privilege, so as to refurbish the claim that the concerned group is in fact *not* repressed and to give substance to the rhetoric of equality among all ethnic groups. Thus, it was always possible, indeed necessary, that certain Swahili individuals occupy the highest position in apparatuses of state while the group as a whole is condemned to insecurity and diaspora.

The politico-economic equation described above applies as much to the Swahili people as it does to other people in east Africa. However, precisely because of the entrenched historical confusion about the identity of the Swahili people, their situation has tended to get substantially aggravated. If the Kamba, the Luo, the Gusii, the Gikuyu, and so forth may feel underprivileged relative to the Kalenjin in Daniel Arap Moi's Kenya, for example, the Swahili feel all the more underprivileged, relative even to the other underprivileged groups, owing to the identity "muddle." It is this sense of extreme underprivilegedness that has continued to augment the numbers of the Swahili *muhajirina* in the Arabian peninsula, in the Scandinavian countries, and more recently in North America. The 1988-1989 wave of Swahili migrants from Kenya to Canada, was so alarming to the Canadian authorities that visa regulations for Kenyan travellers to Canada were soon revised to curb the influx.

If the initial wave of Swahili *muhajirina* from Zanzibar and Pemba was triggered more directly by political persecution, subsequent waves were more a product of economic persecution. Inequality of educational opportunities, reduced chances of employment and promotion, discriminatory practices in workplaces, recurrent instances of economic dispossession, not to mention innumerable humiliating experiences in government offices that offer public service, have all combined to prompt many Swahili people to seek refuge elsewhere in the "vast world of Allah." While all these instances are essentially economic, they acquire a political dimension precisely because they revolve around the struggle for Swahili identity. And, indeed, many of these *muhajirina* have their own concrete politico-economic stories to tell.

While there is a wide range of variation in the details of these *muhajirina* stories, their historical origins are invariably the same. Whether under the centralist tendencies of the Kenyatta government or the *majimboist* (regionalist) tendencies of the Moi government in Kenya, for example, the pattern has always begun with the appointment of non-Swahili to virtually all key positions of state and parastatist institutions, in predominantly Swahili societies. In employment and promotion and in the delivery of crucial services, these state and government functionaries then begin to favor their own kith and kin, their own ethnic compatriots, to the disadvantage of the local Swahili population. The end result is a frustrated, embittered, and alienated community.

More recently, the Moi regime has attempted to promote a few Swahili individuals to positions of limited prominence, to include them, for example, on the boards of directors of certain parastatist organizations. But considering the political context and timing of these appointments, there is reason to believe that they were not intended to redress the long existing problem of Swahili marginality. Their objective, rather, was to contribute to a public impression of broad multiethnic commitments of the Moi administration at a time when it was increasingly being discredited for its strong "tribal" leanings.[28]

It can reasonably be argued, therefore, that the few Swahili individuals who appear to have moved closer to the corridors of power under the Moi regime are mere pawns in its game of survival. At the same time, however, this political need to use the Swahili (and other ethnic minorities) in the regime's quest for a longer lease of life has not terminated generalized Swahili dispossession nor allayed Swahili fears of disenfranchisement, and overwhelming evidence of Swahili peripheralization in the political, economic, and educational spheres of Kenya's national life continues.

Swahili experiences of dispossession have by no means been restricted, moreover, to the professional domain. There have also been instances of collective material disinheritance. Most of these relate to the question of land ownership. Let us look at two specific instances. First, there was the Lake Kenyatta Harambee settlement scheme at a place called Mpeketoni in the predominantly Swahili district of Lamu on the northern coast of Kenya. This scheme was launched in 1970 by the Kenyatta government with the stated objective of producing cotton. The idea was to settle people on ten- to twenty-acre plots to serve as cotton producers. This was the era of a Gikuyu (ethnic) oligarchy, and the settlement scheme, therefore, soon took an ethnic turn. By 1975 over three thousand Gikuyu families had been settled with a provision for yet more to come.

According to Shiva Naipaul, the official government report of the scheme claims to have appealed first to the Swahili people, urging them to take up the "challenge" and agree to be settled in the scheme. Having failed to get any response from the local people, the government decided to look elsewhere for human labor that could set the project in motion. And, of course, in the thinking of the ethnocratic government of Kenyatta, the Gikuyu were the only Kenyans who could supply that labor. In actual fact, however, this was Kenyatta's way of responding to the increasing demand for land from a predominantly Gikuyu peasantry that had been dispossessed and had remained landless in the aftermath of the struggle for independence. Bent on protecting its own kleptocratic interests by refusing to reform Kenya's land policy, and incapable of creating new economic opportunities, the Kenyatta regime was caught in a vicious circle of dispossessing one group of Kenyans in order to fulfill the more assertive demands of another. Just as Idi Amin dispossessed the Indians to create opportunities for Africans in Uganda, Kenyatta now felt he could dispossess the Swahili to provide for an increasingly restless Kikuyu squatter population. So by 1972, according to Naipaul, the government-engineered invasion had begun (1978:190-191).

But that degree of mass dispossession required a legitimating ideology of a sort. This ideology was ready at hand in the pop-

141

ular stereotype of the Swahili as inherently lazy in character. According to Naipaul, the government report accused these coastal people not only of lack of enthusiasm towards the project but also of laziness. The comical presidential depiction (by both Jomo Kenyatta and Daniel Arap Moi) of the Swahili as "lazy bones," who derived their sustenance by passively sitting under coconut and mango trees to wait for fallen fruits, was thus elevated into an ideology that legitimized the dispossession of the Swahili.

Like the colonialists before them, then, the neocolonial kleptocrats found a ready instrument of exploitation in the "ideology of laziness." During colonialism this ideology was used to expropriate African labor. Go-slows, refusal to take employment on colonial farms, were adopted by Africans as hidden forms of protest against settler colonialism. Colonialism, in turn, promoted the image of the African as congenitally lazy in order to justify use of force and coercion to mobilize African labor. As a European humanist once commented:

> We have often heard about the inborn laziness of the Blacks. . . .That is an old and false accusation through which a number of big owners of sugar factories hope to justify lashing their slaves to make them dig. . . .When they refuse to work, it is because they are not paid or because they are mistreated. (Quoted by Kesteloot, 1972:97)

People who had once been victims of this colonialist ideology in Kenya now came to use it to expropriate African land, not African labor. Those called "lazy" were thus deemed undeserving of any land ownership, and a certain kind of developmentalist ideology was mobilized to justify the transfer of that land go to those who have the energy and resolve to till it.

According to the Swahili people of the area,[29] however, the government never seriously tried to interest the local people in participating in the project. The announcements that were made were quite muted. The few people who heard about the project had a host of concerns, including the education of their children, health facilities, possibilities of funding for irrigation, machinery, and fertilizers. But the government officials would not commit themselves to addressing any of these issues. What followed ultimately convinced the local Swahili people that the government was not at all interested in seeking their participation in the project in the first place. It merely wanted to use the alibi of Swahili laziness and lack of enthusiasm to go about infiltrating Swahililand with Kikuyu settlers. It is against this background that we can understand how the new settlers got as a matter of right — funding for a dispensary, schools, church, and irrigation — what the Swahili sought as a matter of clarification.

The Lake Kenyatta Harambee settlement scheme was a case of a Kikuyu oligarchy dispossessing a section of the Swahili people. But there have also been instances of individual members of that oligarchy dispossessing the Swahili in pursuit of their personal kleptocratic interests. This leads us to the second example of collective Swahili dispossession. In his travels along the coast of Kenya, Naipaul narrates his encounter with a "wooly-haired, flat-nosed, thick-lipped" Swahili boy. The lad told him of the utterances of Kenyatta government officials to the effect that one day the Swahili people would be driven back to Arabia (Naipaul, 1978:178). Such statements from top government functionaries were not at all uncommon when addressing Swahili audiences. It was their way of "reminding" the Swahili that they were actually "Arabs," foreigners who had no claim to the land they were occupying. In this way, then, they could justify coming in to grab Swahili land over and over again. Grab! Grab! Grab! The "song" of Arabness had become yet another element in the ideological arsenal intended to dispossess the Swahili people.

The fate of several Swahili peasants from Manda, again in Lamu district, is quite revealing in this regard. One sunny day the Provincial Commissioner (PC) of the coast province, who, it is said, had once served as a "home-guard" for the British colonial government in Kenya, decided to address the people of the district on a range of issues connected with "development." In his address, however, he took advantage of every opportunity to "remind" the people of their "foreignness" for reasons that were not quite apparent to the audience.

It was not until a few months later that the real motives of the commissioner's diatribe dawned on the Swahili people of the area. The "awakening" came when the PC deluded a whole group of Swahili peasants into leaving their land because, they were told, the government needed it for some strategic projects. Thus the PC prepared the path for the dispossession of the peasants by appealing to their patriotic sentiments and their fear of the government. Apparently the PC had made a secret deal to lease that piece of land as private property to an Italian hotelier, popularly known in the area as Bruno, to establish an exclusive club for Italian tourists.[30]

When the peasants finally came to learn the facts of the matter, they tried to resist the move. Led by a certain Bakari Shee Lali, they tried to reoccupy their land but in vain. The police were called in; the peasants were forcefully removed and their leader arrested, temporarily detained and threatened with state action: they were imprisoned without trial. But Bakari Shee Lali was not the kind of person who gave up easily. He made their case known to the newspapers, he got their representative in parliament to raise the matter in the house, and finally he even attempted to take the PC to court.[31] But the kleptocratic politics of neocolonial Kenya militated against any successful resolution of the situation. The Swahili peasants of Manda were thus doomed to an irreversible state of landlessness. Similar, though perhaps less dramatic experiences, can be cited elsewhere on the coast of Kenya.

These land-grab schemes doubtless arise from an admixture of many motives: the privileging of some ethnic groups above others, the forcible eviction of poor peasants by state functionaries and their clients, the intensified capitalist dynamic that has seen land values rise astronomically, and so on. But the public image of the Swahili as an alleged foreigner and of Islam as an alien incursion into African culture surely facilitates a situation where the Swahili can be dispossessed with impunity not only of his general cultural identity but also of his material possessions, while broad sections of the schooled non-Swahili compatriots either remain silent or even applaud the dispossession. This same element of "foreignness" of the Swahili has also been used to justify the complete disregard for the religion of the Swahili people, i.e., Islam. Despite its Islamic character, the Swahili town of Mombasa was once again opened up to American naval personnel, who were expected to visit the islands on a rotational basis from the Saudi Arabian desert to satisfy certain of their social and sexual needs (*New York Times,* Dec. 10, 1990), which the more conservative Islamic environ- ment of Saudi Arabia could not provide. Or President Moi could sanction a major address by Reverend Bonke of Germany in the predominantly Muslim town of Mombasa, while his commis- sioners were proscribing Muslim scholars from Tanzania from addressing the Muslims of the same town. Not suprisingly, this government callousness led to the Mombasa Swahili demon- strations of October 30, 1989.

The marginal status of the Swahili at the domestic front in the last third of the twentieth century seems to contrast sharply, however, with their visibility at the more international level. From the secretariat of the Organization of African Unity to the studios of Western television, from international diplomacy to universal academia, the Swahili community, relative to its pop- ulation size, has demonstrated visible achievements through its sons and daughters. The domestically dispossessed have sometimes been professionally triumphant beyond the confines of their national boundaries.

But how has this Swahili visibility been regarded by the inter- national community of fellow Africans? Generally, quite posi- tively. In 1981 African delegates were united in supporting Salim Ahmed Salim's bid for the United Nations Secretary General's position. Salim is a Tanzanian Swahili from Pemba island. His spectacular performance at the international diplo- matic arena was considered a collective achievement of all African peoples. Similarly, despite its many critics, Ali Mazrui's television series, *The Africans: A Triple Heritage,* has generally been proclaimed a monumental victory for Africa as a whole and a tribute to its genius. True to their African heritage, Africans on the international scene do not seem to have regarded the Arab factor in the ancestral background of these Swahili individuals as a mark of lesser Africanity.

More recently, however, Wole Soyinka, a renowned African scholar and writer, and the first African recipient of the Nobel Prize for Literature, has deviated from this international African tradition. Invoking what are essentially Eurocentric terms of reference, Soyinka seems to regard Ali Mazrui as less African than himself because, in ancestry, Mazrui has Arab affiliations:

> Mazrui . . . is not just culturally Arabized, he is by both blood and vocal identification part Arab. Surely we who have listened to him proudly speak of his Arab lineage have a right to refer to it in a relevant context. . . .We can propose, objectively, that Mazrui says this or does this because his cultural roots are also forged in the Arab hearth. *The Africans* was not a series made by a black African. . . .(180)

This is an extraordinary statement. From Somalia and Sudan to Algeria and Mauritania, there are more African Arabs than there are non-African Arabs in all the rest of the world, and they come in all kinds of pigmentations. How *black* does one have to be in order to be counted as "black"? The habit of counting the percentages of "white" and "black" blood particles in the veins of human beings is a relic, one would think, of the slave codes in the American South and of the *apartheid* in South Africa. But one only has to be a Swahili, it appears, to be subjected to that kind of blood count. If Ali Mazrui truly goes around boasting about his Arab lineage only, then he must certainly be accused of alienation and intellectual dependency. But does he have to obliterate a part of his lineage in order to lay claim to the country and the continent to which he has always belonged. Even if Ali Mazrui were to take exaggerated pride in the Arab part of his lineage, that would hardly warrant regarding him as non-African, as Soyinka does. After all, mental dependence that has led many Africans to view the "self" in terms of the "other" is, especially among the middle and upper classes, a continent-wide phenomenon. The tendency to regard skin pigmentation and "bloodline" as the central criteria of identity is steeped in the racist muddle of Eurocentricism. The resulting irony is that Mazrui's *Africanity* is questioned by Soyinka on the basis of *Eurocentric* terms of reference!

Posing the question of Mazrui's Africanness in the particular Eurocentric manner that Soyinka does also arms the European North with a dangerously divisive weapon against global Africanity and against the underlying unity of the African Diaspora. African Americans, for example, are keenly conscious of their Africanness despite the cultural and genetic infusion from Europeans. Indeed, according to Cavalli-Sforza, African Americans, on the average, derive thirty percent of their gene pool from people of European ancestry (110). To Soyinka, this would amount to a dilution of the Africanness of African Americans, a negation of the "blackness" of their Africanity. If Mazrui's Africanness is seen as questionable, despite the fact that he is a direct product of Africa in geographical, genetic, linguistic and cultural terms, then, in Soyinka's eyes, African Americans, who have been geographically and linguistically alienated from the continent and are genetically infused with Europeans, would have little right to their cherished claim to African identity.

Be that as it may, sentiments like those of Soyinka are unlikely to influence the international African community. The destiny of the Swahili people is still primarily at the mercy of domestic politics in east Africa. The domestic background we have provided so far allows us not only to understand the increasing numbers of the *muhajirina* abroad, but also the growing sentiments of resistance among the Swahili people. From Mombasa to Zanzibar, from Lamu to Tanga, the Swahili have been turning to Islam for inspiration, resistance, and collective self-preservation. Islam has now come to provide a basis not only of positive reaffirmation of Swahili identity, but also a basis of regenerating the glory of an honorable past that inspired the Swahili resistance against the Portuguese. In the process some Swahili have even converted to Shi`ism, which they consider to be a more militant brand of Islam. This growing section of the Swahili population has been arguing that pacifism, not fighting back against oppression, is itself a sin.

The emerging pattern is clear. The more dispossessed the Swahili become through the denial of their identity, the more nationalist they become about that identity and the more radical their response. The era of the popular stereotype of the Swahili as a politically "passive" people may therefore be coming to an end as the neocolonial politics of marginalization and disenfranchisement increasingly prompt them towards both the religious and the secular kinds of militancy.

The strong inclination of Eurocentric scholarship to emphasize the "Arab" element in Swahili identity, however, does not affect the political and economic destiny of the Swahili people alone. It also has far-reaching implications for the African continent in general. This conclusion follows from the obvious double standards of Eurocentric scholarship in defining the ethnic or "racial" identity of the "other."

In the introductory chapter we suggested that the Eurocentric paradigm of identity would normally regard an offspring with anything less than a hundred percent "European blood" as belonging to the "other." Thus, an offspring who, over a period of several generations, has come to have a genetic pool that is predominantly European and only marginally African, for example, would still be regarded as African.

This Eurocentric standard has been compromised frequently, however, by some European scholars when dealing with the Swahili people. The Arab element is often given primacy over the African element despite the fact that the boundary between the two is, at best, quite fuzzy. The offspring of European-African intercourse is not seen to have lost its Africanity or to have shifted towards Europeanness by even the slightest degree. The offspring of Arab-African intercourse, on the other hand, as many members of the Swahili community happen to be, are automatically regarded as de-Africanized to some degree or other. How then do we explain this inconsistency in Eurocentric scholarship?

Our position here is that this double standard is, in fact, not unrelated to the long history of Eurocentricism to dispossess "others" of their genius and heritage. For a long time, the typical Eurocentric view of Africa, for example, was that of a dark continent inhabited by an illiterate, ignorant people, living under primitive conditions and having no developed sense of artistic creativity. With the Swahili history of literacy, learning, and scholarship, an impressive architecture, and rich poetic tradition and so forth, Swahili society turns out not to fit neatly into this European stereotype. Rather than accept these achievements as products of African genius, prompted and influenced, no doubt, by contact with the "external world," Eurocentricism is inclined to regard them as essentially non-African in origin. The two-nature theory of the Swahili, which makes them only partly African and partly — even predominantly — Arab, is part and parcel of this disappropriative agenda of Eurocentricism.

The Eurocentric response to the Swahili can be likened, though to a smaller extent, to the Eurocentric response to ancient Egypt. For a long time Eurocentric scholarship had claimed that ancient Egyptian civilization was non-African, supposedly because "racially" ancient Egyptians were more "Caucasoid" than "Negroid." It has now been shown beyond doubt that this was a manifest distortion of the people's history. No doubt there were "non-Africans" from the Mediterranean belt who settled in Egypt and interacted with the local population. However, in time, these "foreigners" were assimilated and acquired an Egyptian, an African, identity. But contrary to the Eurocentric paradigm of identity prevalent in European societies, Eurocentricism inverted this equation by de-Africanizing Egypt in genetic and cultural terms. In this way, then, the heritage of Egypt could be conveniently appropriated.

There is a sense, then, in which the nationalist resistance against the dis-Africanization of Egypt and against the de-Africanization of the Swahili, in Eurocentric scholarship, is part and parcel of that wider intellectual struggle to reclaim Africa's heritage in all its multifarious manifestations.

AFTERWORD
ISLAM AND SWAHILI
ETHNO-NATIONALISM

 the completion of the manuscript of this book events have unfolded in Kenya which essentially vindicate our position —namely, that the Swahili have been victims of economic dispossession and political marginalization partly in consequence of the prevailing prejudices against their Islamic affiliation, and that the systemic nature of their prolonged subordination is leading to the gradual radicalization of, at least the younger members of the community.

In this regard, one of the most significant events was, perhaps, the one-day civil strike that took place in Mombasa, Kenya's second largest city, on May 24, 1993. This action virtually paralyzed the entire city as schools and offices remained closed throughout the day and businesses and transport companies withheld their services from the public. The provincial office of the government of Kenya did what it could to undermine the strike, using a series of stick-and-carrot strategies, but to no avail: At the end of the day it was heralded as the most successful strike in Kenya since the country attained independence in 1963.

Unlike many other civil actions in the history of Kenya, however, this strike was not the work of the trade union movement nor of any major political party in the opposition. It was organized, rather, by a relatively small and unregistered group under the name of the Islamic Party of Kenya (IPK) in protest against the Kenya government's bias in, and interference with, the administration of justice. The IPK was concerned that Muslim leaders were being singled out for prosecution for alleged offenses of "incitement of the public," even though the actions for which they were being persecuted were no different than similar acts of opposition undertaken by leaders of other communities in the country.

What surprised many Kenyans and puzzled many a political analyst, however, was the extent of the success of the IPK-inspired strike. There were probably two factors behind this achievement. One was the fact that the IPK enjoyed tremendous popular support in Mombasa. In a sense, Mombasa was the party's political stronghold; and the undemocratic decision of the Kenya government not to register it, ended up strengthening rather than weakening the organization, especially in terms of political resolve, internal radicalization of the organization itself as well as the degree of social sympathy that IPK gained in opposition to the government's obviously discriminatory refusal to register it as a legitimate organization.

But equally important in the success of the strike was sheer fear of an IPK backlash against strike-breakers. Indeed, just a day before the event the city was flushed with leaflets urging people to support the strike and, at the same time, giving potential strike-breakers a stern warning of impending "retaliatory" measures. The government's assurance that it would position para-military units throughout the town to protect those who chose to go to work against IPK threats of violence only exacerbated the already highly charged atmosphere and increased the sense of insecurity. The possibility of a deadly confrontation between the para-military and IPK supporters, therefore, further convinced potential strike-breakers that their personal security lay in "supporting" the strike even if inadvertently.

Long before this event, however, the IPK had already established a national reputation of militancy and of using counter-violence when provoked, in their struggle for democratization (or what some observers have termed Kenya's post-colonial struggle for liberation). Several Swahili youths were shot to death in recurrent street confrontations with the "anti-riot" police, some buses of companies that defied IPK's advise against ferrying Swahili women to Nairobi to dance for President Daniel arap Moi were set ablaze, and police stations and the district headquarters of the ruling party, the Kenya African National Union (KANU), became targets of petrol-bomb attacks. It is this mood of militant defiance, sometimes at the risk of one's life, that led Professor Ali Mazrui to describe the protest as a potential "Black Intifadah" (*The Weekly Review*, July 9, 1993, p.6), as a Kenyan version of the Palestinian uprising against occupation and discriminatory policies of the government.

What, then, was the essence of this militant activism of Mombasa's Muslim community? Was it a reflection of the more global Islamic "fundamentalist" upsurge, or was it a response to something more local? Our contention here is that while the "IPK syndrome" was given a moral boost by the dynamics of international Islam, it was primarily an Islamic expression of Swahili ethno-nationalism. What had hitherto been repressed in a politically-closed climate, and articulated only in whispers behind the scenes, suddenly burst open into the streets of Mombasa with a radicalism that took the entire Kenyan nation by complete surprise. Commenting on the state of violent confrontation in Mombasa, Mukalo wa Kwayera remarked:

> The Muslims have since independence been a very peaceful community but, as it is beginning to unravel now, behind the peace and quiet, and apparent docility, lay frustration and an urge to fight for their rights at whatever cost. (*Society*, June 29, 1992, p. 9)

In other words, with Islam as their inspirational force, the Swahili were no longer willing to accept a second class citizenship status in a country where they have all along contributed significantly in the political, economic and cultural domains.

But in what sense can the citizenship status of the Swahili be described as second class? Politically, the Swahili, and Muslims, in general, have been highly under-represented in the country's executive institutions, both national and local, even in areas where they constitute the overwhelming majority. Key administrative positions of the government in predominantly Swahili towns like Mombasa, Lamu and Malindi, are virtually all held by the non-Swahili from upcountry Kenya. This preponderance of the non-Swahili in the available job market is supplemented, then, by a pattern of development— or, lack of development— in which the over-all rate of unemployment at the Swahili coast is approximately twice the national average (*Society*, June 29, 1993, p. 10). The Swahili suffer, in other words, from double jeopardy: much slower rate of job creation in their region as compared to other regions of the country, and the propensity to award most of the existing jobs to the upcountry non-Swahili. Considering that the civil service is still the largest single employer in Kenya, it is not unreasonable to attribute this state of chronic underemployment and unequal employment on the coast, at least in part, to lopsided employment policies of the Kenya government.

In the epilogue we also had occasion to describe a couple of concrete incidents of economic dispossession of the Swahili. But that is only the tip of the iceberg. Since November 1993, the clandestine Islamic Research Center in Mombasa has been releasing weekly leaflets providing specific and detailed information on the massive amount of looting that has been carried out in the district by highly placed political figures, again mainly from upcountry Kenya.

It is this combination of political and economic factors that is increasingly leading to calls for *Majimbo*, a Swahili word for regionalism that refers to a semi-federalist arrangement that would empower people in different parts of the country to have some control over their own resources and destiny. *Majimbo* has thus come to be seen as one possible way of weakening the kleptocratic hold over the Swahili coast by a ruling class that is essentially non-Swahili. Expressing this sentiment Professor Ali Mazrui, for example, writes:

> As someone who comes from the Kenya coast, I have seen over the years the wealth of the coast passing from Coastal hands into the hands of the "upcountry citizens" with tribal connections in the central government in Nairobi. Under both President Jomo Kenyatta and President Daniel arap Moi the coast has been, quite literally, looted by non-coastal Kenyans. Who owns the best land at the Coast? Who runs the best hotels? Who controls the tourist industry at the Coast? Who enjoys the best jobs? Even a relatively superficial scrutiny will soon reveal the overwhelming domination of non-coastal names.

This is a condition of domination that Professor Ali Mazrui describes as internal colonization, leading him eventually to proffer political and economic *majimbo* as a solution to the problem (Ali Mazrui, 1993:3-4).

The question that now arises is the following: If the political upsurge at the Coast of Kenya is truly an expression of Swahili ethno-nationalism, why has its prominence been concentrated in Mombasa, and why has it assumed a peculiarly religious, i.e. Islamic, orientation?

While the Swahili themselves are a numerically small community, what is called the Swahili coast is dotted with several towns that are primarily Swahili in ethnic composition. Among these, Mombasa holds a special place for historical as well as geographical reasons. First, Mombasa is the most cosmopolitan among the Swahili towns. Having served as the country's capital during the early years of British colonialism, and being one of the largest cities in Kenya, it has attracted rural-to-urban migrants from various parts of the country. All these people have come to Mombasa with their own peculiar attitudes towards the Swahili, some of which are very negative and assume a particularly oppressive character when held, as they often are, by functionaries of the state. The Mombasa Swahili have repeatedly complained about harassment from police constables, for example, most of whom happen to be non-Swahili. The weight and effects of oppressive attitudes of out-groups towards the Swahili, therefore, were perhaps more pronounced in Mombasa than in other less cosmopolitan Swahili towns.

Related to the cosmopolitan character of Mombasa, is its status as the provincial headquarters of the Coast where all the key administrative posts of the provincial government are based. Again, virtually all these posts of power and authority are held by non-locals. In government offices, therefore, the Mombasa Swahili are constantly confronted with a picture and an attitude that reaffirms the disproportionate distribution of political power and the bitter reality of their political marginalization.

Furthermore, Mombasa is a major port city in the region, serving not only Kenya, but also several other countries in east and southern Africa, and brings in millions of dollars' worth of merchandise and revenues. It has, thus, offered Kenyans not only employment opportunities but also investment opportunities in transportation, import and export trade, and clearing and forwarding services. But instead of going to the local population, these investment opportunities have ended up in the hands of non-locals, often with the complicity and assistance of the state.

Mombasa is also a favorite tourist town, and in most years, tourism is rated as number one foreign exchange earner in the country. Again, non-Swahili and non-Coastal Africans have often used powerful political connections at their disposal to grab prime beach properties, establish hotel businesses and control the tourist industry. In essence, then, the kleptocractic exploitation of the city's port and tourist status has given rise to a state of economic inequality in favor of non-local Kenyans that is more glaring in Mombasa than in other towns.

The concentration of the above economic and political factors, then, have perhaps made the Mombasa Swahili experience the "liabilities" of their ethnicity in Kenya's political equation to a much greater extent than Swahili communities elsewhere on the Coast. Dialectically, therefore, Mombasa had all the politico-economic ingredients in high enough concentrations to trigger Swahili ethno-nationalism earlier and more prominently than in the rest of the Swahili coast. If Mombasa was one of the earliest Swahili towns to resist external domination (by the Portuguese), it has now become the first Swahili town to resist internal domination (by Kenya's ethnocrats).

The conditions that allowed Swahili ethno-nationalism to be more pronounced in Mombasa are, of course, quite local. The conditions that led to the Islamization of Swahili ethno-nationalism, on the other hand, are more national. As indicated in Chapter One, Islam as a culture is an essential accompanying attribute of Swahili identity. It is perhaps conceivable to have a Swahili person who is not a Muslim in religious faith; it is, however, less conceivable to have a Swahili individual who is not a Muslim in cultural practice. The place of Islam in Swahili ethnicity, however, while indispensable, is not sufficient to explain why Swahili ethno-nationalism took a religious expression. The other necessary ingredient was the sectarian politics of the Kenya government, especially in the era of President Daniel arap Moi. Our proposition here is that Swahili ethno-nationalism assumed a religious expression primarily in response to the quasi-theocratic or, specifically, Christocentric nature of the Kenya government.

What, then are some of the manifestations of this alleged centrality of Christian influences in Kenya's politics? One of these is attitudinal and has its roots in the legacy of missionary education. As we tried to demonstrate in Chapter One Christian missionary education peddled certain images of Islam and Muslims that have left an indelible mark in the minds of the East African elite of Christian faith. What shocked many Kenya Muslims, however, was the discovery that these anti-Islamic sentiments prevailed even in the highest echelons of the state. This was demonstrated by President Moi himself when, in a Madaraka Day address on June 1, 1992, he reminded non-Muslim Kenyans, in a typical colonial-missionary style, that Islam and Muslims had been responsible for the enslavement of their forefathers (*Society*, June 29, 1992, p.11). These kinds of sentiments which put the Islamic dimension of Swahili identity on the defensive, were bound to thrust Islam to the foreground of Swahili resistance to internal domination.

Another important manifestation of the identification of Kenyan national ethos with Christian identitarian assertion is to be found in that definition of the national ideology which has been propagated under the banner of *Nyayoism* since 1978 when Daniel arap Moi assumed the reigns of presidential power—though, it is only fair to add, out of no democratic choice on the part of Kenyan citizens at large. Though political in nature, this ideology is at least partially rooted in the Christian faith and heavily inspired by Christian precepts. In the words of President Daniel arap Moi himself, *Nyayoism* "singularly embeds the kernel of the principles of Christian life into the national philosophy" (1986: 36). The Christian element in the *Nyayoist* approach to public affairs is, in fact, intended to pervade the entire spectrum of Kenya's national life.

Yet, when some Kenyans decided to form the Islamic Party of Kenya, the organization was refused registration with the explicit intervention of the president. Kenyans were, thus, forced to accept a national ideology "fired by the eternal concepts of a living Christianity," but denied the freedom to choose a party with an Islamic-based ideology. All this underscored the Christian bias of the *Nyayoist* status quo, a condition which could easily prompt a counter-ideology of a religious nature.

The *Nyayo* ideology, then, provided additional conditions for the Islamization of Swahili ethno-nationalism.

Finally, the Christian bias in the politics of Kenya is also manifested in specific, overt and covert policies of the government, as the following should illustrate.

First of all, there has long been in Kenya a colonially inspired and politically motivated equation of Islam with "foreign origin" and "non-Africanness" that has served to rationalize government attempts to deny Muslims certain of their fundamental rights as citizens and to relegate them to a state of chronic disempowerment. Muslims are not only highly under-represented in key institutions of the state and government, there is evidence that they have sometimes been subjected to discriminatory practices when they seek to apply for national identity cards and passports. In the area of passports applications, in particular, by the end of 1992 Muslims were still required to produce additional documentary evidence of citizenship. While Christian applicants only needed two birth certificates, their own and of one of their parents, applicants with Islamic names were required to produce, in addition, the birth certificate of one of the grandparents.

The presence of refugees from the predominantly Muslim Somalia has sometimes been used to justify this unconstitutional practice. The same treatment, however, has never been extended to Christian Kenyans on account of refugees from predominantly Christian regions of Africa. For instance, there has long been an influx of Nilotic speaking refugees, carrying Christian names, from neighboring Uganda and Southern Sudan. Yet there has not been any government action to subject Nilotic speaking Kenyans of the Christian faith to this discriminatory exercise of having to produce additional evidence of citizenship. The impression that has been created, then, is that immigration policies and practices of the Kenya government are designed to favor Christians, allowing them to take their Kenyan citizenship for granted to a greater extent than can Muslim Kenyans.

In the educational sphere, meanwhile, there have been charges of a pattern of inequality in the provision of essential services, facilities and opportunities that has effected the Muslims adversely. In Mombasa, the second largest city in

Kenya, for example, the majority of government sponsored elementary schools that have performed the poorest in the national examination happen to be predominately Muslim. Predominately Muslim schools that have performed relatively well have been privately owned, by and large. Educationally, therefore, Muslims in Kenya seem to be relatively underprivileged.

Muslims in Kenya have also enjoyed unequal access to the means of mass communication. The Kenya Broadcasting Corporation (KBC) television, in particular, has continued to demonstrate a pro-Christian bias despite the fact that it is funded by a tax-paying public which includes a significant section of members of the Islamic faith. In addition to irregular programs, events and scenes of Christian orientation that appear on KBC television, there have been as many as six regular Christian programs each week. These have included *Joy Bringers, Sing and Shine, Nyimbo Za Dini, Sunday Music Parade, Invitation to Happiness* and *700 Club*. On the other hand, until December 1992, there was no attempt on KBC's part to establish even a single program to accommodate the religious interests of its non Christian viewers. And when the government eventually allowed Muslims to have one half-hour program a week, it was clearly intended to be a pre-election campaign strategy to woo Muslim voters for KANU. The government-owned television media, then, has continued to give the impression that electronically too Kenya is a Christian country that barely tolerates a Muslim presence.

These are but a few examples of a pro-Christian bias in the very conduct of the political and not-so-political affairs of Kenya whose cumulative impact may have been the increasing Islamization of Swahili ethno-nationalism. The contention of this afterword, then, is that it is precisely this pro-Christian bias of the dominant power bloc in Kenya under Moi's rule that has led to the politicization of religion, a trend that has partly expressed itself in the formation of political parties like IPK. It is also this same Christian bias which has given the Swahili their ethno-nationalist democratic struggle a strong Islamic inclination turning them into the most militant supporters of IPK.

In sum, then, if the many years of ethnocratic domination, on the one hand, and politico-economic disfranchisement, on the other, have eventually led to the upsurge of Swahili ethno-nationalism, the sectarian tendencies of Kenya's leadership have helped to Islamize its political thrust. In the process, and in the context of the new political space that has been created by the pro-democracy movement, more and more facts have come to light that reveal the nature and extent of the plight of the Swahili in particular and of the Muslims in general. But, instead of trying to come to terms with this state of affairs and seeking a political solution to it, President Moi's regime has been more inclined towards commandism, blind repression and naked display of force. The end result of this iron-handed government response to the expression of legitimate grievances, however, has been the increasing radicalization of Swahili ethno-nationalism, aided in its spirit of resistance by the international dynamics of a resurgent and militant Islam.

As in Kenya, there is some indication that Tanzania too is beginning to experience a militant Muslim assertion. The Tanzanian situation is, of course, somewhat more complex than that of Kenya. As indicated in Chapter One, this complexity is owed partly to the "union" arrangement between Zanzibar and what was once Tanganyika, partly to the fact that Swahili as an identitarian category has been "nationalized," and partly to the impression that religion rather than ethnicity has all along been the more central consideration in the country's power politics.

There have long been Muslim protestations in mainland Tanzania, for example, that their right of association has been infringed upon by the government of the *Chama cha Mapinduzi* (CCM). Muslims in mainland Tanzania have had a strong desire to form an Islamic organization which would cater for their religious and social needs. Until recently the only Islamic body that was legally empowered to represent Muslim interests was BAKWATA (Baraza Kuu la Waislamu wa Tanzania - i.e. the Supreme Council of Tanzania Muslims) which, in the eyes of many Muslims was a sheer imposition, formed by the government of Julius Nyerere in 1968 as an instrument of the state to control rather than to provide for them. (*Mizani*, May 7, 1993, p. 2). This ultimately led to a confrontation between the government and sections of the Muslim population when, in 1993, the latter sought to register "their own" religious-cum-welfare organization, BALUKTA (Baraza la Uendelezaji wa Kurani Tanzania -Council for the Advancement of Koranic Education in Tanzania), all in consonance with the spirit of pluralism that has been developing in the country.

The urge to form a new body controlled by Muslims rather than by the state (as BAKWATA allegedly was and continues to be) is predicated upon the feeling that, as a country, Tanzania is under the influence of the church (*Mizani*, May 7, 1993, p.8) and is not positively inclined towards the advancement of its Muslim population. As in Kenya, therefore, the alleged preferential treatment of Christians over Muslims in Tanzania is generating increasing radicalization among members of the Islamic faith. In the words of an Islamic socio-political gazette of Kenya, "What actually lies beneath all this is Muslim resentment towards the CCM government for allowing itself to be controlled by Christians who over the years have become insensitive to Muslim grievances" (*The Message*, June 1993, p. 8).

As indicated in the epilogue, in Zanzibar too there have been strong sentiments that a predominantly Christian-controlled CCM has imposed its rule, quite undemocratically, on a predominantly Muslim population. Many Zanzibaris opposed to the union with Tanganyika (or mainland Tanzania), therefore, have turned to Islam as a source of nationalistic assertion. This trend of events is probably what partly led Zanzibar to join the membership of the Organization of Islamic Countries (OIC) - an act which in the eyes of the CCM government almost amounted to a unilateral declaration of independence. This Zanzibari decision raised so much uproar from mainly Christian politicians from mainland Tanzania and generated so much political tension between the two federal states, that Zanzibar was ultimately pressured to withdraw from OIC (*Mzalendo*, August 15, 1993, p. 1). For many Tanzanian Muslims all this was a further reaffirmation of their political powerlessness, and of the political power wielded by a Christian oligarchy.

Despite the ups and downs of the Islamic-inspired protest movement in both Zanzibar and Mombasa, however, the two predominantly Swahili towns demonstrated in no uncertain terms the potentially critical role of Islam as a force of resistance and unity among the Muslims who feel beleaguered in countries which continue to be defined in terms of Christian

161

dominance and even exclusivity by their respective states. And it is partly in response to this state of political affairs that some pro-establishment politicians in both Kenya and Tanzania have resorted to divisive symbols of an extra-religious nature in an attempt to undermine the protest.

In Zanzibar this divisive measure has come in the form of public pronouncements by some functionaries of CCM like Omar Aweso Dadi in support of some of the atrocities committed by the then government of Sheikh Abeid Amani Karume supposedly against Zanzibaris of Arab ancestry. Arab ancestry, real or imagined, is once again being projected as a liability, as a symbol of an intrusive "other." In the new climate of political pluralism those Zanzibaris who express a democratic opposition to CCM are now "looked upon by the government and CCM leaders as *invaders* rather than Tanzanians who are merely practicing their birth and democratic rights" (*Family Mirror*, May 1993, p. 14). And to cap it all the same issue of *Family Mirror* reports how the spirit of the pre-union, "anti-Arab" Afro-Shirazi Party is being revived, again, seemingly by functionaries of CCM.

In Mombasa, on the other hand, the seeds of divisiveness wrought by the revival of the racialist spirit of Afro-Shirazi, have been planted by the formation of the United Muslim of Africa (UMA), in July 1993. This body, which is generally regarded as a front for KANU has the declared objective of fighting against IPK which, in its opinion, is dominated by Swahili people of Arab ancestry (*Africa Confidential*, 34.21, 1993:7). Unlike the experience of all other unregistered organizations in Kenya, UMA has several times been licensed, by the government, to hold public meetings at which inflammatory racist speeches are delivered. According to *Africa Confidential* (34.21, 1993:7), the UMA-KANU objective is seemingly to kill IPK by injecting into Mombasa and coastal politics the same kind of quasi-ethnic bloody conflict that has been perpetrated in the Rift Valley region of the country.

In sum, then, events in both Kenya and Tanzania indicate that if the "fuzziness" about Swahili identity was once used to legitimize their dispossession and marginalization, it has now become a convenient tool to break their Islamic-inspired protest against their continued economic and political disfranchisement. But only time can tell whether or not Islam as an inspirational force of a united protest will ultimately win over the divisive machinations that are being continually hatched in the region.

ENDNOTES

1. The terms "Eurocentric," "Afrocentric," "Arabocentric," and so forth are used here to refer to different conceptual tendencies in approaching the world of human relations. Different presuppositions inform these different tendencies. This does not mean, however, that all Europeans are necessarily Eurocentric or all Africans necessarily Afrocentric in their approaches to human society. A European scholar, for example, may begin with presuppositions or with a set of axioms that render his approach quite Afrocentric.

2. Shorn of its negative connotations *tribe* could be a useful technical term to refer to the self-contained, self-governing, internally cohesive societies prior to the emergence of the "nation-state." The nation-state tends to compromise this self-containment, self-governance, and internal cohesion. The nation-state, in other words, tends to recreate the tribe into something new, into a *nationality*. A term very much akin to nationality is *ethnic group*. The main difference between the two is that whereas members of a nationality are associated with a coterminous geographical unit, permitting the use of terms like Kikuyuland or Swahililand within Kenya, those of an ethnic group are not. When the geographical boundaries of a nationality coincide more or less completely with the geographical boundaries of the state, then the nationality would have become a *nation*. Technically, therefore, *nationality* would be the most suitable term for our discussion of Swahili identity. But because nationality is popularly used to refer to citizenship in a particular nation-state, we shall opt for

the term ethnic group. Ethnic group and nationality will, therefore, be used as synonyms in this discussion.

3.   This part of the world constitutes the larger section of what is often called the Middle East. While Aribocentricity may be a tendency of this entire region, there is within it another model, the Arabiancentric paradigm, which is more exclusively characteristic of the Arabian peninsula. In the latter case, language and culture are not sufficient nor even necessary features of Arabian identity. More significant a factor is paternal lineage. Several generations of a person's ancestry may have been physically located outside the Arabian peninsula and may even have been assimilated into the language and culture of their new home. But as long as the individual can trace his/her patrilineal ancestry to the Arabian peninsula s/he would be a bona fide Arabian in identitarian terms.

4.   There were African societies, of course, like the Baganda and the Amhara, that had developed economic modes less communal and more akin to feudalism before the inception of European colonial rule.

5.   With this awareness of its power the European world also began to project its own *particular* paradigm, its Eurocentric paradigm, as a universal absolute. Eurocentric paradigms were given a scientistic aura that went beyond the boundaries of particular cultures and social experiences. The fetish of objectivity was partly created to deceive the world that the "European particular" is a "human universal."

6.   In our discussion about the Swahili we shall be using the terms "Arab" and "Arabian" more or less interchangeably. As indicated earlier, the majority of Arabs are, in fact, Africans. But the Arabs with whom the Swahili have maintained lasting historical contacts are mostly Arabians, i.e., a section of Arabs located in the Arabian peninsula. It is possible to argue, of course, that the Arabian peninsula itself was part of Africa before the great rift. But we shall limit ourselves to the present geographical configuration,

bearing in mind that cartography was itself informed by politico-economic motives. The decision to make Africa end at the Red Sea rather than at the Arabian/Persian Gulf was made, after all, neither by Africans nor by Arabs, but by European cartographers and mapmakers (Mazrui, 1986:23).

According to the above considerations, then, the term Afro-Arab or African-Arab would be a misnomer if it is intended to refer to some relationship between people of north Africa and those of what is at times called Sub-Saharan or "black" Africa. Afro-Arab or African-Arab would be a meaningful term only if used in connection with peoples of the African continent in relation to Arabs located in Asia. By extension, then, pan-Arabism can legitimately be considered an Afro-Arab phenomenon, but continental pan-Africanism cannot. Continental pan-Africanism, a current that includes predominantly Arab countries of north Africa, would simply be an African phenomenon.

7. The supporters of the Swahili included both the Mijikenda and a section of the Omani Arabs. The Omani assistance was based not only on historical commercial ties and a shared religion, but also being a common enemy with the Portuguese. According to Nicholls:

> At the beginning of the sixteenth century the Omanis' contacts with East Africa had assumed a more significant aspect when their own coastline, like that of East Africa, had been conquered by the Portuguese. Already sharing a common commercial interest, the Omanis and the inhabitants of the East African littoral now faced a common enemy. In 1650 the Omanis were able to recapture Muscat, their major seaport, from the Portuguese. (21)

By assisting the Swahili in liberating their land from Portuguese rule, therefore, the Omanis hoped to strengthen the resistance against any further Portuguese incursions against Oman and to free the Indian Ocean from the tolls and restrictions imposed by the Portuguese.

8. The periodization of Eurocentric scholarship with regard to the Swahili coast must be recognized as no more than an exercise in the enumeration of *average* tendencies of the time. At any one period there were several and sometimes conflicting views competing with each other. But it is also possible to isolate one or two tendencies in every period that could be said to have been more characteristic and to have influenced policies at the time.

9. In discussing slavery in the Muslim world, Ali Mazrui comments:

    > Slavery as practiced in the Muslim world was multiracial. Both the masters and the slaves could be almost of any race. An Arab master could own slaves who came from Africa, Europe or Asia. Indeed, the Arab master could also own Arab slaves, Turks owned Syrian slaves, and Syrians owned Indian and Greek slaves. Although slavery as practiced by Muslims often included prejudice against this or that ethnic group or caste, skin-colour was not the central divide between masters and slaves. There was no theory which characterized one race as natural slaves and another as natural masters. The slave system in the Muslim world was not rooted in a basic philosophy of racial stratification, as was the case with the trans-Atlantic slave trade. (1990: 2)

10. It is often forgotten that the great majority of Africans who were forced into captivity by Arabs were, in fact, destined for European markets. There is a sense in which, like many African peoples but to a lesser degree, Arabs served as middlemen in the European trade in African "human cargo." But, by a twist of history, the middle-men now came to be projected as the real culprits, while the controlling traders, the European slave traders, were made to fade into oblivion. In the annals of east African history, specifically, a great colonial brainwashing exercise was launched that could lead Africans to remember Europeans only as saviors and not as slavers. It is in this respect that

Alpers (1967:4) criticizes Marsh and Kingsnorth (1957) for perpetuating the British colonial point of view of the east African slave trade through the various editions of their book, *An Introduction to the History of East Africa,* which until recently was the standard school textbook in east Africa.

11. The term "Hamitic" has been rejected by most postcolonial African historians. The term "Cushitic" is now used in its place.

12. In Europe, linguistic consolidations, aided by "print capitalism," played an important, constitutive role in the emergence of nation-states.

13. The notion of race has now been proven to be completely devoid of any substance, and Sapir's position essentially reflects the Eurocentric attempt to apply nineteenth century race theory to linguistic formations.

14. There is no doubt that at this point Swahili language and culture maintained an Islamic spirit. But what was now happening was the superimposition of a Eurocentric ideology of racial linguistics on an existing, though by no means an invariable and immutable, fact in east Africa.

15. By the phrase "Swahili nationalists" we mean those Swahilis who display a passionate attachment to the idea of a delimitable Swahili nationality with emphasis on its historical commonality with other African nationalities in the region. Its central tendency is essentially reactive, seeking to counteract the Arab bias in Swahili studies, with a reaffirmation of Swahili's Africanity.

16. These are merely presumptions based on the *impressions* of the Greek author of the *Periplus.* These impressions may have been wrong: the Arabs, for example, may have understood several, mutually intelligible languages of the coast; but the Greek author may have been convinced that the people were speaking one language. On the other

hand, the Greek author's impressions may have been accurate, in which case the assumptions of his statement that the Arabs "understood their language" would be valid.

17. In this technique there is a set of tape-recorded voices, reading the same passage, to which experimental subjects are asked to respond. The first and last voices are of the same person but in two different guises — in this case, one in standard Swahili and one in Kimvita. In this way, the technique achieves control on voice and content, and allows the respondents to react essentially to the dialects or languages being investigated. The technique is not without its problems and weaknesses, but it is known to be one of the most effective instruments for the study of language attitudes that social psychology has devised thus far.

18. This is a near literal translation of an excerpt from a July 1990 interview with John "Mtembezi" Innis, editor of *Ufumbuzi*. *Ufumbuzi* is a Swahili journal with a pan-African focus published in Washington D. C. by the editor.

19. We define a national language here as that language spoken widely across ethnic boundaries in a particular country, even if officially it has not been accorded such a status.

20. We acknowledge the fact that, oftentimes, it is not easy to specify what would constitute genuinely secular literature in Swahili. As a whole among the Swahili, verbal discourse is so often saturated with phrases like *akipenda Mola* (if God wills) and *rehema ya Mungu* (God's mercy) that it becomes difficult to draw a sharp distinction between the sacred and the secular in verbal culture. However, the scholars who suggest that Swahili "traditional" poetry is wholly religious, usually refer to themes. In our opinion, by contrast, the use of phrases with religious origin need not render a poem thematically nonsecular.

21. Though William Hichens appears as the editor of Muyaka's anthology, the actual collection of Muyaka's verse is attributed by many Swahili notables to Mwalimu Sikujua of Mombasa.

22. There is, of course, a distinction between blank verse and free verse. Blank verse dispenses with rhyme but not with meter, while free verse dispenses with both. However, to the best of our knowledge, there is as yet no evidence of Swahili poetic compositions in blank verse. Poets who have experimented with a mode other than the prosodic one have generally tended to compose in free verse.

23. We are using the term prosody in this context to refer specifically to the features of meter and rhyme since other prosodic attributes of Swahili poetry do not seem to have been featured in the debate on Swahili poetic form.

24. We have used the terms "conservationist" and "liberalist" to avoid the political, ideological connotations in the more common usage of the terms "conservative" and "liberal." Conservationists are those who advocate the preservation of the poetic "status quo," and liberalists are usually proponents of experimentation with new poetic form. Neither of the two groups can be said to be homogenous in terms of political-ideological persuasion. The conservationist school is comprised of members who range, in political terms, from radical to conservative. The liberalist school includes politically liberal-minded scholars, even though its most vocal advocates have so far been ideologically to the left.

25. At another level of analysis, one cannot do justice to this topic without pointing out that this entire debate is somewhat class-bound. It is in a sense an intellectual tussle between a more "traditional" Swahili intellectual elite and a modern intellectual elite, despite the fact that their words are couched in terms of concern for the "common man." In practice, the collective-functional poetry of the common man, like the so-called *ngonjera* poetry of Tanzania,

entails virtually no linguistic problems of accessibility either at the level of diction or metaphor.

26. John Okello was a Ugandan resident in Zanzibar who was publicized as one of the key leaders of the revolution in its early phases.

27. For more details see the feature article, "The 100 Days That Made Tanzania" in *Africa Now*, April 1984, pp. 15-21 and Amrit Wilson, 1989.

28 See the editorial in *The Nairobi Law Monthly*, Number 30, February 1991.

29. Much of the information used in discussing Lamu/Manda experiences is based on personal interviews with a wide cross-section of Lamu people who have requested anonymity.

30. In 1982, one of the authors, Alamin Mazrui, travelled to Manda with a friend from Kenyatta University and some members of the dispossessed family of Bakari Shee Lali with the explicit objective of talking to Bruno about the whole affair. Bruno refused to discuss the matter, however.

31. Bakari Shee Lali had a whole file of correspondence with government officials and lawyers on the Manda affair and gave us complete access to it, for which we are grateful.

BIBLIOGRAPHY

Abdalla, Abdilatif. *Sauti ya Dhiki*. Nairobi: Oxford University Press, 1975.

Abdulaziz, Mohamed H. *Muyaka*. Nairobi: Kenya Literature Bureau, 1979.

Abedi, Kaluta Amri. *Sheria za Kutunga Mashairi na Diwani ya Amri*. Dar es Salaam: East African Literature Bureau, 1965.

Africa Now (April 1984):15-21.

Allen, J. de V. "The Swahili World of Mtoro bin Mwinyi Bakari." *The Customs of the Swahili People*. By Mtoro bin Mwinyi Bakari. Ed. and tr. J. W. T. Allen, Berkeley: University of California Press, 1981.

Allen, J. W. T. "The Rapid Spread of Swahili." *Swahili* 30 (1959):15-22.

—— *Tendi*. London: Heinemann, 1971.

Alpers, E. A. *The East African Slave Trade*. Historical Association of Tanzania, paper No. 3. Nairobi: E.A.P.H, 1967.

Amin, Samir. *Eurocentricism*. New York: Monthly Review Press, 1989.

Arnold, Rainer. "Swahili Literature and Modern History: A Necessary Remark on Literary Criticism." *Kiswahili* 42.2 and 43.1 (1973):68-73.

Arens, W. "The Waswahili: The Social History of an Ethnic Group." *Africa* 45.4 (1975): 426-38.

Bernal, Martin. *Black Athena: The Afroasiatic Roots of Classical Civilization.* New Brunswick, N.J.: Rutgers University Press, 1987.

Cavalli-Sforza, Luigi Laca. "Genes, Peoples and Languages." *Scientific American* (November 1991):104-110.

Childers, Erskine B. *Common Sense About the Arab World.* London: Victor Gollanes Ltd. 1960.

Chiraghdin, Shihabuddin. "Utangulizi." (Foreword) *Utenzi wa Fumo Liyongo.* By Muhammad Kijumwa. Ed. Abdilatif Abdalla. Dar es Salaam: Chuo cha Uchunguzi wa Lugha ya Kiswahili, 1973. i-iv.

—— "Utangulizi." (Foreword) *Malenga wa Mvita.* By Ahmed Nasir. Nairobi: Oxford University Press, 1971. 3-24.

—— "Kiswahili na Wenyewe." *Kiswahili* 44.1 (1974):48-53.

—— "Kiswahili: Tokeya Ubantu Hadi Ki-`Standard Swahili.'" *Kiswahili* 44.2 (1974):14-18.

—— "Utangulizi." (Foreword) *Sauti ya Dhiki.* By Abdilatif Abdalla. Nairobi: Oxford University Press, 1974. ix-xii.

—— and Mathias Mnyampala. *Historia ya Kiswahili.* Nairobi: Oxford University Press, 1977.

Chittick, Neville. "The Coast Before the Arrival of the Portuguese." *Zamani.* Ed. by B. A. Ogot and J. A. Kieran Nairobi: East African Publishing House, 1969: 100-18.

Cohen, John. *Africa Addio.* New York: Ballantine Books, 1966.

Cory, H. *Sikilizeni Mashairi.* Mwanza: Lake Printing Works Ltd, 1958.

Coupland, R. *East Africa and its Invaders*. London: Oxford University Press, 1938.

Darroch, R. G. "Some Notes on the Early History of the Tribe Living on the Lower Tana, Collected by Mikael Samson and Others." *Journal of the East African Natural History Society* 17.3-4, 77–78 (1943): 244–54.

Davidson, Basil. *Africa in History*, New York: Macmillan, 1991.

——— *A History of East and Central Africa*. New York: Doubleday, 1969.

——— *Africa*, A Mitchel Beazley Television, MBT/RM Arts/Channel Four Co-Production. New York. 1984.

Diop, Cheikh Anta. *The African Origin of Civilization*. Newport, CT: Lawrence Hill, 1974.

Eastman, Carol M. "Who are the Waswahili?" *Africa* XLI. 3 (1971): 228–36.

Freeman–Grenville, G. S. P. *The East African Coast*. Oxford: Clarendon Press, 1966.

Harries, Lyndon. *Swahili Poetry*. Oxford: Clarendon Press, 1962.

Heine, Bernd. *Pidgin-Sprachen im Bantu-Bereich*. Berlin: D. Reimer, 1973.

Hichens, W. *Diwani ya Malenga wa Waswahili*. Unpublished manuscript, 1939.

——— *Diwani ya Muyaka bin Haji Al–Ghassaniy*. Johannesburg: University of Witwatersrand, 1940.

Horton, Mark. "The Swahili Corridor." *Scientific American* 257 (1987): 86-93.

Hughes, A. J. *East Africa: The Search for Unity*. London: Penguin African Library, 1962.

Hyder, Mohamed. "Swahili in a Technical Age." *Contemporary African Monograph Series Number 4: East Africa's Cultural Heritage*. Nairobi: The East African Institute of Social and Cultural Affairs (1966): 78-87.

Kenyatta, Jomo. *Facing Mount Kenya*. New York: Vintage Books, 1965.

Kesteloot, Lilyan. *Intellectual Origins of the African Revolution*. Washington, D.C.: Black Orpheus Press, 1972.

Kezilahabi, E. *Kichomi*. Nairobi: Heinemann, 1974.

Kiango, S. D. and Sengo T. S. Y. "Fasihi." *Mulika* 4 (1972):11-17.

Kirkman, J. S. *Men and Monuments of the East African Coast*. New York: Frederick A. Praeger, 1966.

Knappert, J. *Traditional Swahili Poetry*. Leiden: E. J. Brill, 1967.

—— *Swahili Islamic Poetry*. Vol. 1. Leiden: E. J. Brill, 1971.

—— *Four Centuries of Swahili Verse*. London: Heinemann, 1979.

—— *Epic Poetry in Swahili and Other Languages*. Leiden (The Netherlands): E.J. Brill, 1983.

Krapf, J. Lewis. *Travels, Researches and Missionary Labours*. London: Johnson Reprint Corporation, 1968.

Lambert, H. E. "Ode to Mwana Mnga," *Bulletin of the Inter-territorial Language Committee* 23 (1953): 56-65.

Lodhi, Abdulaziz, Y. "Language and Cultural Unity in Tanzania." *Kiswahili* 44/2 (1974):10-13.

Bibliography

Lofchie, Michael F. *Zanzibar: Background to Revolution.* Princeton: Princeton University Press, 1965.

Madan, A. C. *Swahili-English Dictionary.* London: Oxford University Press, 1903.

Marsh, Zoe and Kingsnorth, G. W. *An Introduction to the History of East Africa.* London: Cambridge University Press, 1957.

Marshad, Hassan. "An Approach to Code Elaboration and its Application to Swahili." Ph.D Thesis. Urbana-Champaign: University of Ilinois, 1984.

Mayoka, J. M. *Mgogoro wa Ushairi na Diwani ya Mayoka.* Dar es Salaam: Tanzania Publishing House, 1986.

Mazrui, Sheikh Al-Amin B. Ali. *Al-Islah.* Mombasu (Kenya) 1931.

Mazrui, Alamin. "Acceptability in a Planned Standard." Ph.D. Thesis. Stanford: Stanford University, 1981.

Mazrui, Ali. A. "Abstract Verse and African Tradition." *Zuka* (Sept. 1967): 13-2.

------ *The Africans: A Triple Heritage.* Boston: Little Brown and Co., 1986.

------ *The Africans: A Triple Heritage.* Television Series. London: B.B.C., 1986.

------ "Political Sex." *Transition* 4.17 (1964): 19-23.

------ "Comparative Slavery and Africa's Triple Heritage." Keynote Address at the World Conference on Slavery and Society in History. Arewa House, Kaduna, Nigeria. March 26-30, 1990.

------ "Magimbo: Political, Economic and Military." Unpublished paper, 1993.

Mazrui, Muhammad Kasim. *Historia ya Utumwa Katika Uislamu na Dini Nyingine*. Nairobi: The Islamic Foundation, 1970.

Mbele, Joseph L. "The Identity of the Hero in the Liyongo Epic." *Research in African Literatures* 17.4 (1986):464–473.

Mbotela, James. *Uhuru wa Watumwa*. London: Sheldon Press, 1934.

——— *The Freeing of the Slaves in East Africa*. Tr. C. G. Richards. London: Evans Brothers, 1956.

Mohamed, Mwinyihatibu. *Malenga wa Mrima*. Dar es Salaam: Oxford University Press, 1977.

Mohamed, Said Ahmed. *'Sikate Tamaa*. Nairobi: Longman, 1981.

Moi, Daniel T. arap. *Kenya African Nationalism: Nyayo Principles and Philosophy*. Nairobi: McMillan. 1986.

Msami, Hassan. "Posho si Sembe." *Mwangaza wa Lugha* 1 (1988): 15-16.

Mulokozi, M. M. "Revolution and Reaction in Swahili Poetry." *Kiswahili* 45.2 (1975): 46–65.

——— "Ushairi wa Kiswahili ni nini?" *Lugha Yetu* 26 (1975)

——— "Protest and Resistance in Swahili Poetry 1660–1885." *Kiswahili* 49.1 (1982): 25–51.

——— and Kahigi, K.K. *Kunga za Ushairi na Diwani Yetu*. Dar es Salaam: Tanzania Publishing House (1979?).

Nabhany, Ahmed Sheikh and Kamal Khan, M. "Swahili: A Challenge to Kenya." *Coast Week* (November 23-30, 1978):6.

Nasir, Sayyid Adallah bin Ali. *Al-Inkishafi*. Nairobi: Oxford University Press, 1972.

Nassir, Ahmed. *Malenga wa Mvita*. Nairobi: Oxford University Press, 1971.

Naipaul, Shiva. *North of South*. New York: Penguin Books, 1981.

Nurse, Derek and Spear, Thomas. *The Swahili: Reconstructing the History and Language of an African Society, 800-1500*. Philadelphia: University of Pennsylvania Press, 1985.

Odinga, Oginga. *Not Yet Uhuru*. New York: Hill and Wang, 1967.

Ohly, Rajmund. "Dating of the Swahili language." *Kiswahili* 42.2 and 43.1 (1973):15-23.

——— "Literature in Swahili." *Literatures in African Languages*. Ed. B.W. Andrzejeweski et al. Cambridge: Cambridge University Press, 1985. 460-92.

Philipson, Robert. "Swahili Literature and Identity: The East African Debate." Unpublished manuscript, 1990.

Prins, A. H. J. *The Swahili Speaking People of Zanzibar and the East African Coast*. London: International African Institute, 1961.

Richards, C. G. "Foreword." *The Freeing of the Slaves in East Africa*. By James J. Mbotela. London: Evans Brothers, 1956. 5.

Robert, Shaaban. *Masomo Yenye Adili*. London: Nelson, 1967.

Rollins, Jack D. "Early 20th Century Swahili Prose Narrative Structure and Some Aspects of Swahili Ethnicity." *Towards African Authenticity, Language and Literary Form*. Ed. Eckhard Breitinger and Reinhard Sander. Bayreuth, W.G.: Bayreuth African Studies 2 (1985):49–68.

Salt, H. *A Voyage to Abyssinia and Travels*. London. 1814.

Samatar, Said, S. "Differing Views of the Swahili." Unpublished manuscript, 1989.

Samoff, Joel. "Pluralism and Conflict in Africa: Ethnicity, Interest and Class in Africa." Paper presented to the International Political Science Association. Rio de Janeiro. August 9-14, 1982.

Sapir, Edward. "The Nature of Language." *Selected Writings of Edward Sapir in Language, Culture and Personality.* Ed. David G. Mendelbaum. Berkeley: University of California Press, 1963.

Sengo, Tigiti. "Utangulizi." *Ushahidi wa Mashairi ya Kiswahili.* By Kandoro, S.A. Dar es Salaam: Longman Tanzania, 1978. iv-ix.

Senkoro, F.E.M.K. "Tenzi za Kiswahili." *Umma* 6.2 (1976): 116–31.

—— *Ushairi: Nadharia na Tahakiki.* Dar es Salaam: Dar es Salaam University Press, 1988.

Shariff, Ibrahim Noor. *Tungo Zetu.* Trenton, N.J.: Red Sea Press, 1988.

—— "The Liyongo Conundrum: Reexamining the Historicity of Swahilis' National Poet," *Research in African Literatures* 22.2 (1991):153-67.

—— "Knappert's Tales." Kiswahili 41.2 (1971): 47–55

Sheriff, Abdul. *Slaves, Spices and Ivory in Zanzibar.* London: James Currey, 1987.

Simiyu, Henry. "Attitudes towards Kiswahili and Waswahili." Unpublished manuscript, 1981.

Soyinka, Wole. "Triple Tropes of Trickery." *Transition* 54 (1991): 179-83.

Steere, Edward. *Swahili Tales.* London: Bell and Daldy, 1870.

Stigand, Captain C. H. *The Land of Zinj*. London: Frank Cass & Co. Ltd., 1913.

Strandes, Justus. *The Portuguese Period in East Africa*. Nairobi: East African Literature Bureau, 1961.

Strayer, Robert, W. *The Making of Mission Communities in East Africa*. London: Heinemann, 1978.

Taasisi ya Uchunguzi wa Kiswahili. *Kamusi ya Kiswahili Sanifu*. Dar es Salaam: Oxford University Press, 1981.

The Encyclopaedia Britannica. XXXVI, Cambridge University Press, 1911.

Todd, Loreto. *Pidgins and Creoles*. London: Routledge and Kegan Paul, 1974.

Tolmacheva, Marina. "The Origin of the Name `Swahili'." *Tanzania Notes and Records* 77 and 77 (1976): 27-37.

Topan, Farouk. "An Approach to the Teaching of Swahili Literature." *Swahili* 38.2: 1968.

—— "Modern Swahili Poetry." *Bulletin of the School of Oriental and African Studies* 37.1 (1974): 175-187.

Velten, C. *Sitten und Gebrauche der Suaheli*. Gottingen: Dandenhoed Ruprecht, 1903.

Werner, Alice. *Myths and Legends of the Bantu*. London: Frank Cass and Co. Ltd., 1968.

Whiteley, W. *The Dialects and Verse of Pemba*. Kampala: East African Swahili Committee, 1958.

—— *Swahili: The Rise of a National Language*. London: Methuen and Co., 1969.

Wilson, Amrit. *US Foreign Policy and Revolution: The Creation of Tanzania*. London: Pluto Press, 1989.

Wright, Marcia. *German Missions in Tanganyika 1891-1941*. Oxford: Clarendon Press, 1971.

Index

The Swahili